ELTON JOHN

Cover photo © Getty Images / Steve Jennings / Contributor

ISBN 978-1-5400-5946-8

Visit Hal Leonard Online at
www.halleonard.com

Contact us:
Hal Leonard
7777 West Bluemound Road
Milwaukee, WI 53213
Email: info@halleonard.com

In Europe, contact:
Hal Leonard Europe Limited
42 Wigmore Street
Marylebone, London, W1U 2RN
Email: info@halleonardeurope.com

In Australia, contact:
Hal Leonard Australia Pty. Ltd.
4 Lentara Court
Cheltenham, Victoria, 3192 Australia
Email: info@halleonard.com.au

Welcome to the *Super Easy Songbook* series!

This unique collection will help you play your favorite songs quickly and easily. Here's how it works:

- Play the simplified melody with your right hand. Letter names appear inside each note to assist you.
- There are no key signatures to worry about! If a sharp ♯ or flat ♭ is needed, it is shown beside the note each time.
- There are no page turns, so your hands never have to leave the keyboard.
- If two notes are connected by a tie ‿, hold the first note for the combined number of beats. (The second note does not show a letter name since it is not re-struck.)
- Add basic chords with your left hand using the provided keyboard diagrams. Chord voicings have been carefully chosen to minimize hand movement.
- The left-hand rhythm is up to you, and chord notes can be played together or separately. Be creative!
- If the chords sound muddy, move your left hand an octave* higher. If this gets in the way of playing the melody, move your right hand an octave higher as well.

* *An octave spans eight notes. If your starting note is C, the next C to the right is an octave higher.*

ALSO AVAILABLE

Hal Leonard Student Keyboard Guide HL00296039

Key Stickers HL00100016

Bennie and the Jets

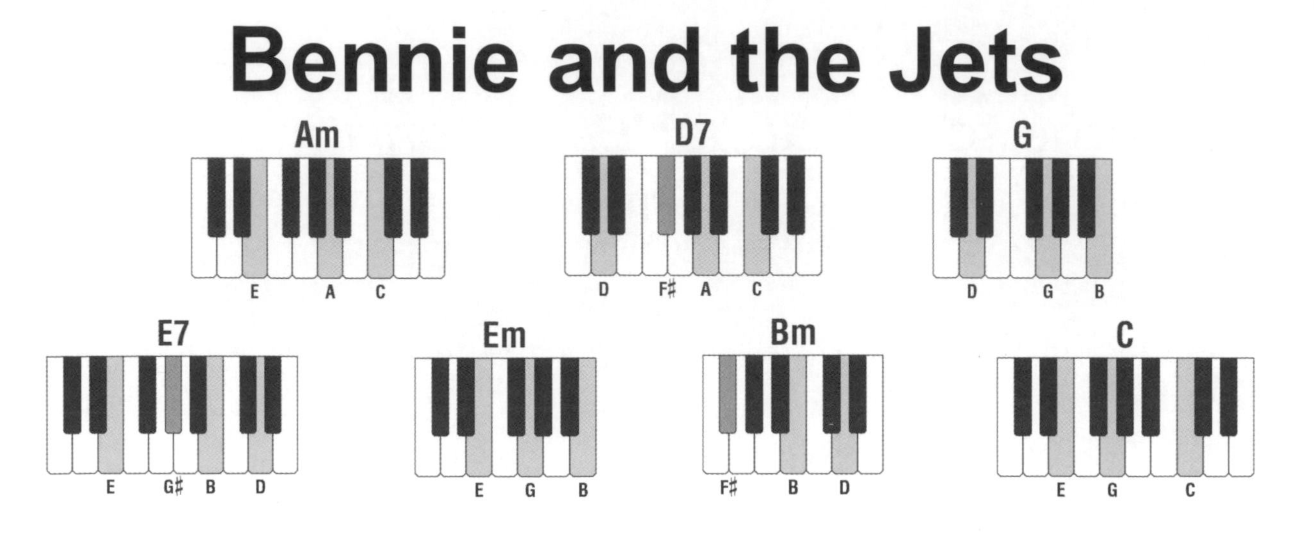

Words and Music by Elton John
and Bernie Taupin

Moderate Rock beat

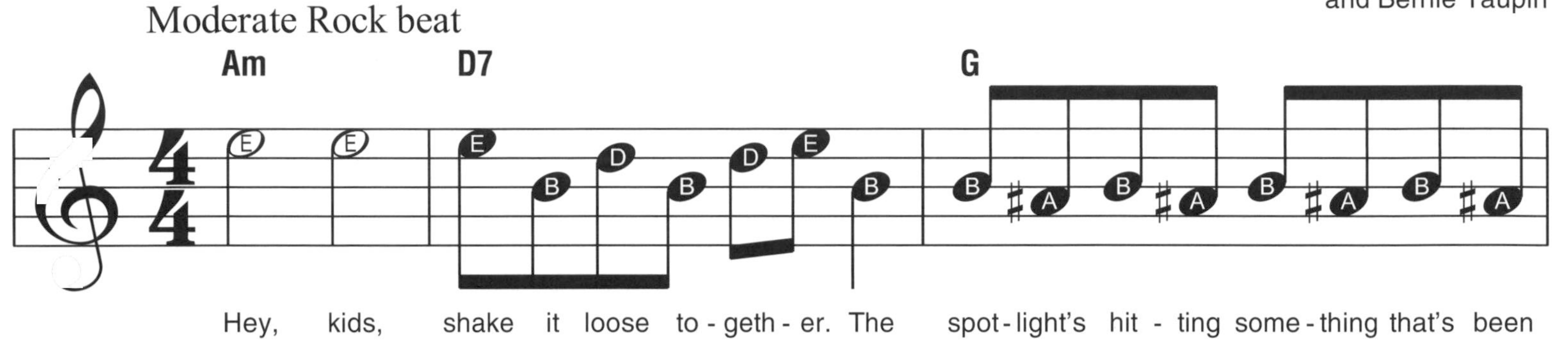

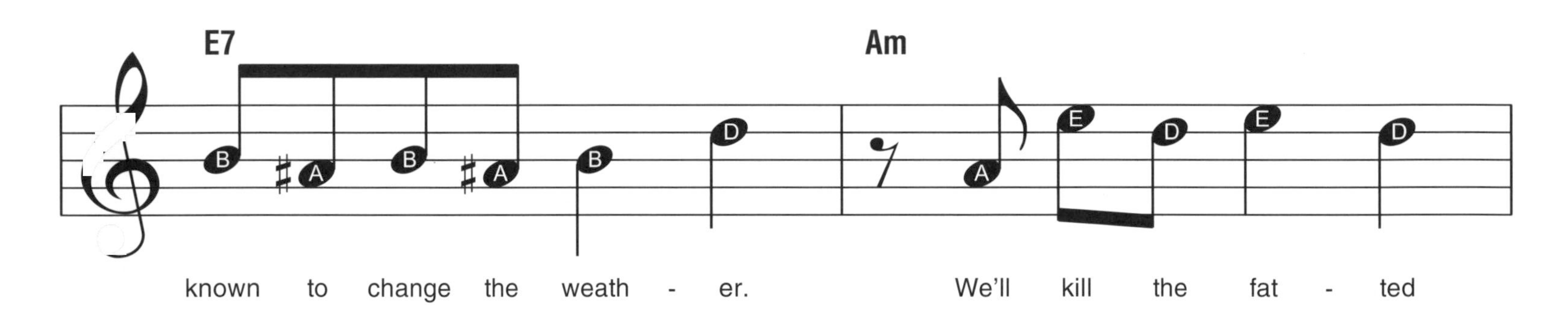

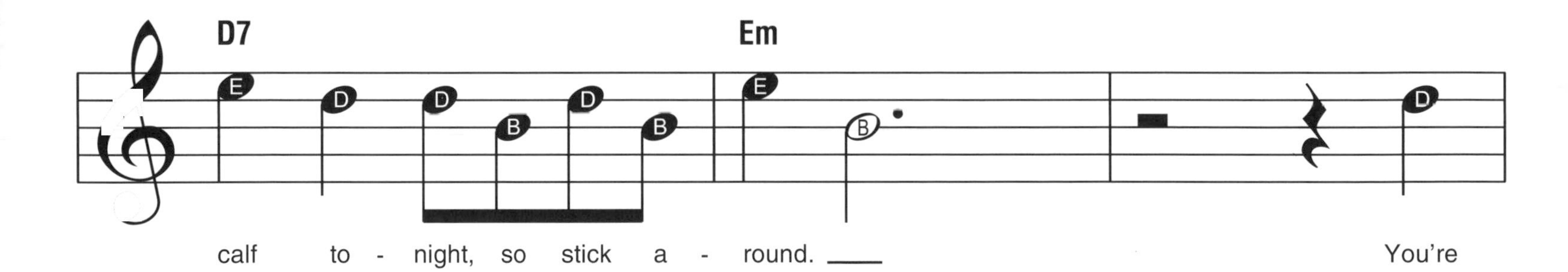

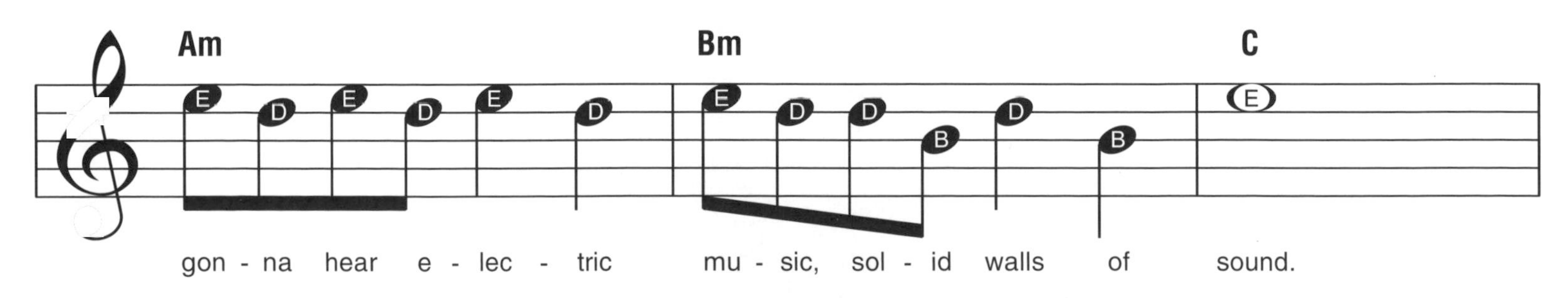

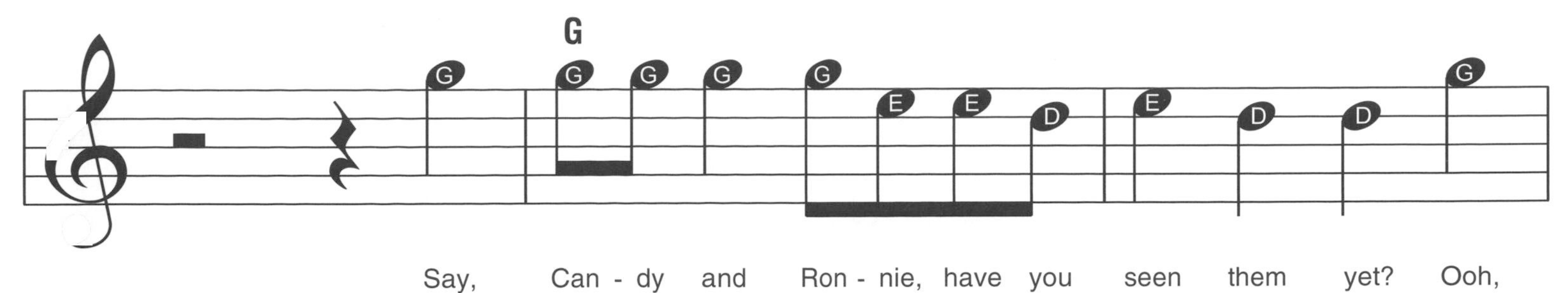
G
Say, Can - dy and Ron - nie, have you seen them yet? Ooh,

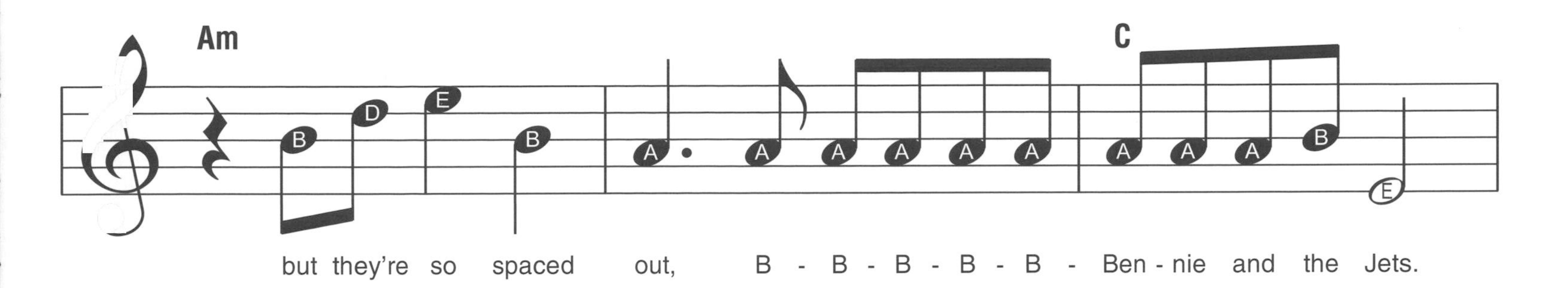
Am
C
but they're so spaced out, B - B - B - B - B - Ben - nie and the Jets.

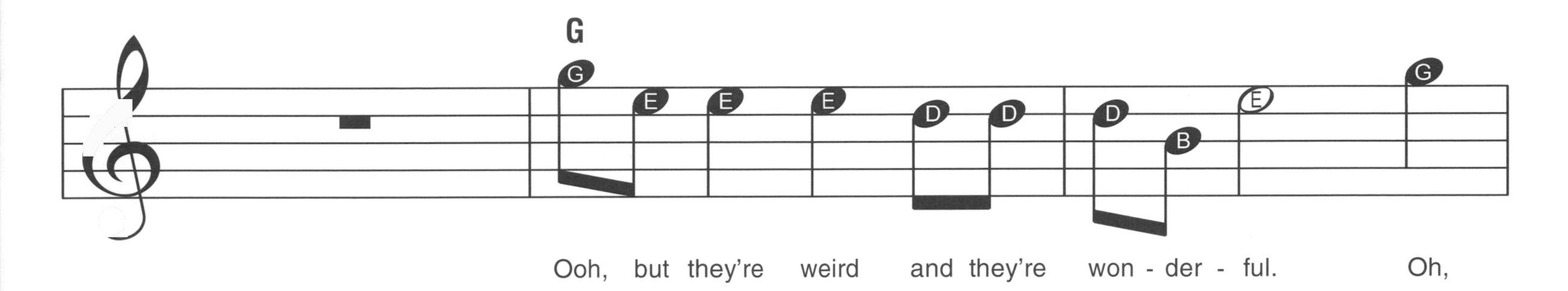
G
Ooh, but they're weird and they're won - der - ful. Oh,

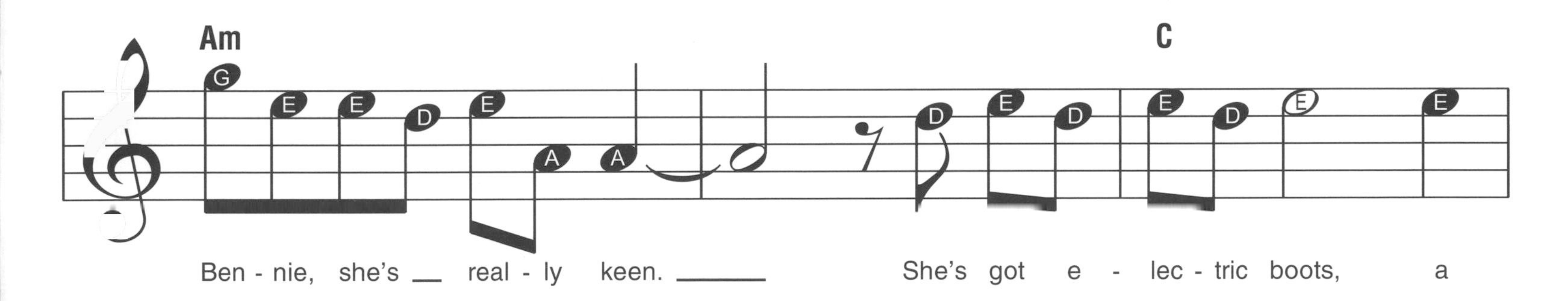
Am
C
Ben - nie, she's real - ly keen. She's got e - lec - tric boots, a

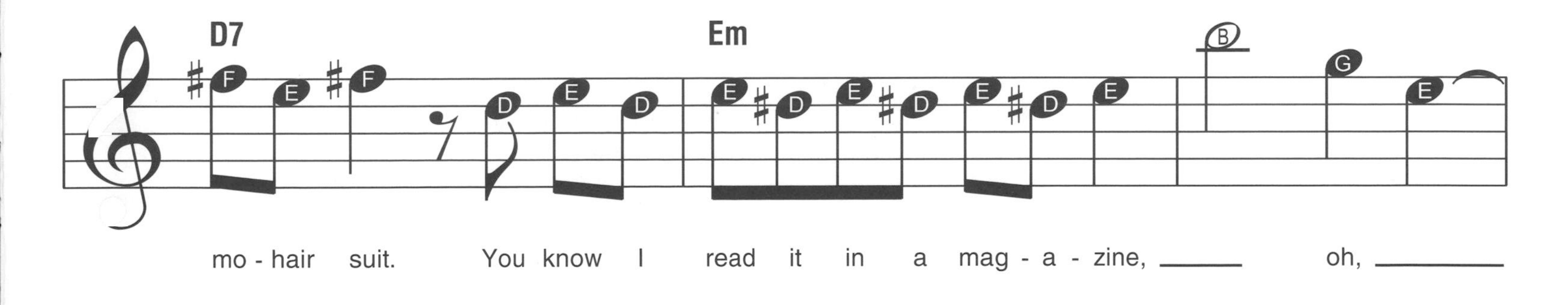
D7
Em
mo - hair suit. You know I read it in a mag - a - zine, oh,

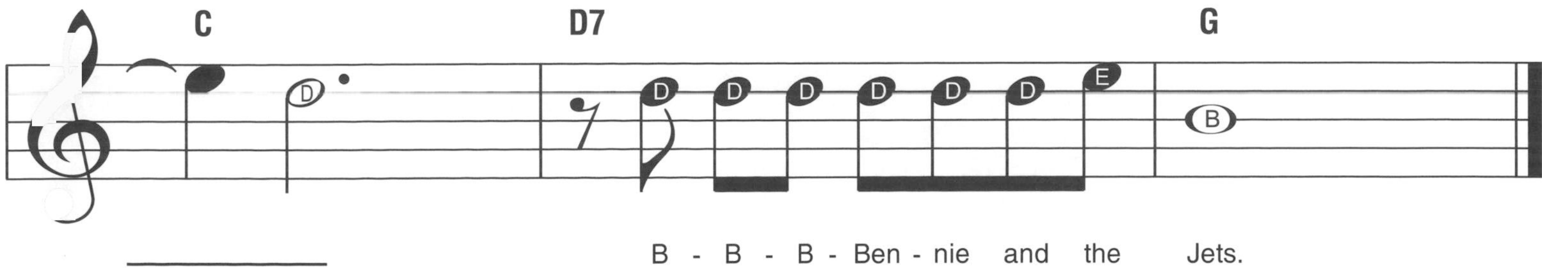
C
D7
G
B - B - B - Ben - nie and the Jets.

Can You Feel the Love Tonight

from THE LION KING

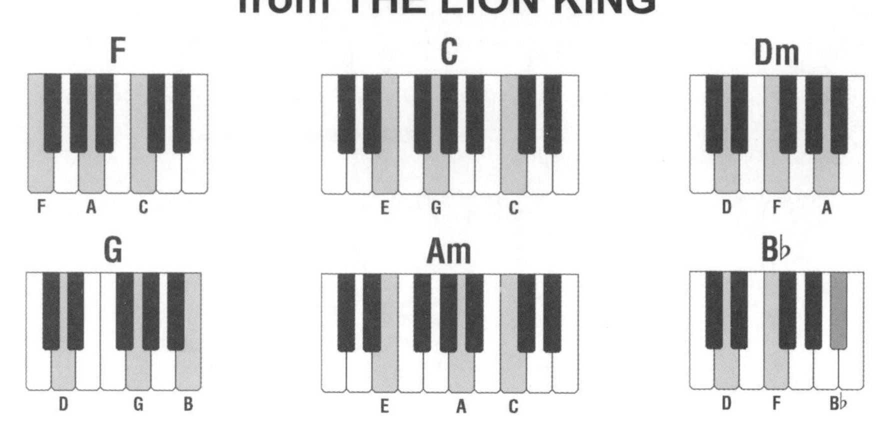

Music by Elton John
Lyrics by Tim Rice

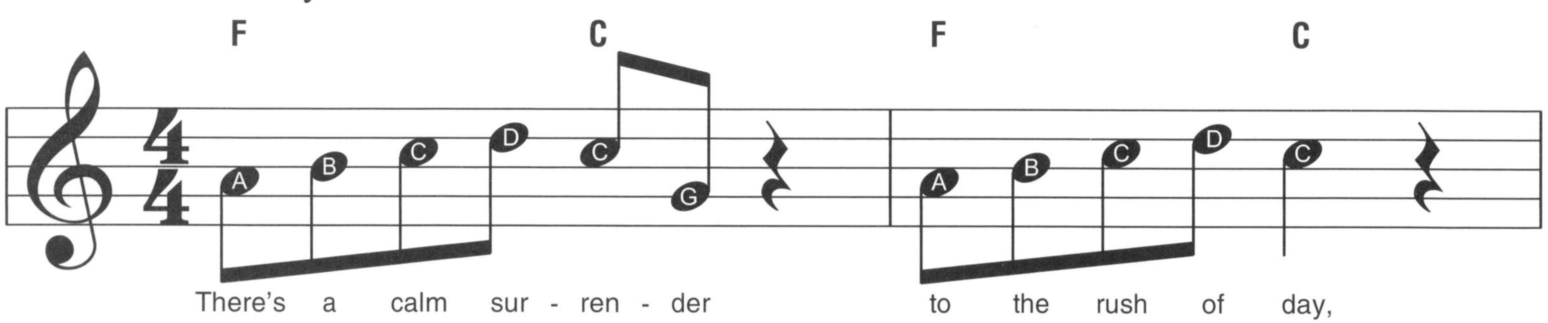

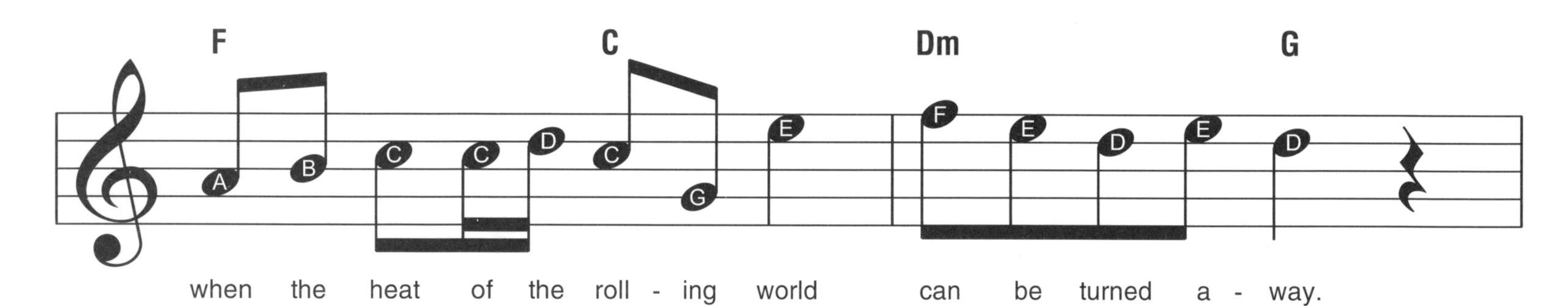

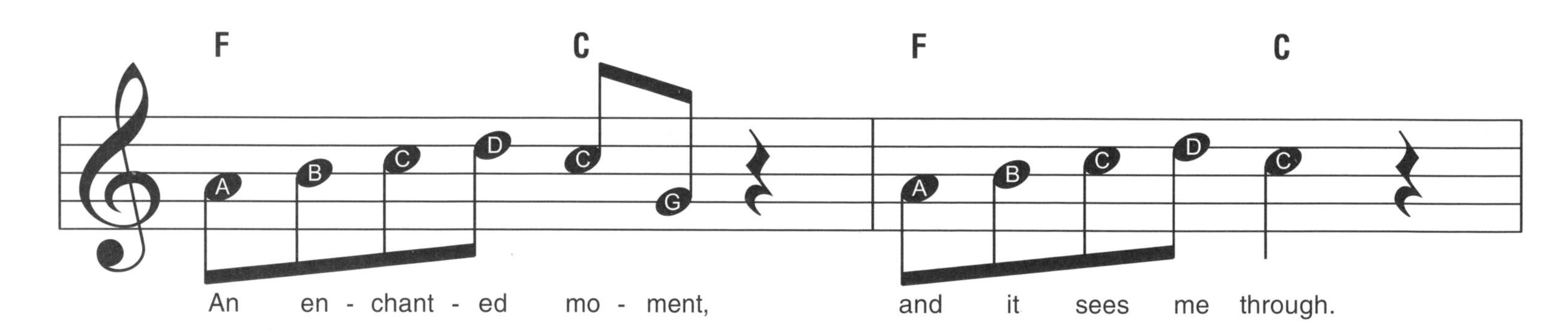

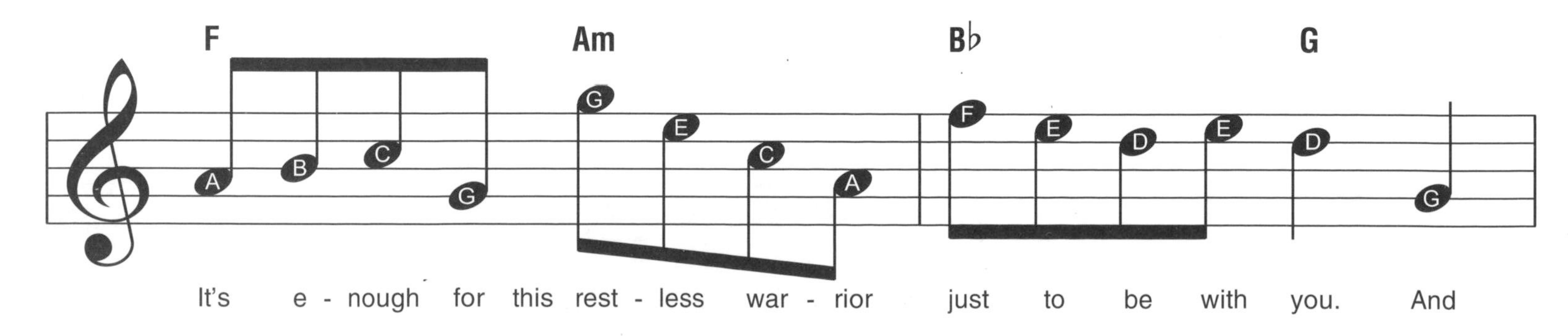

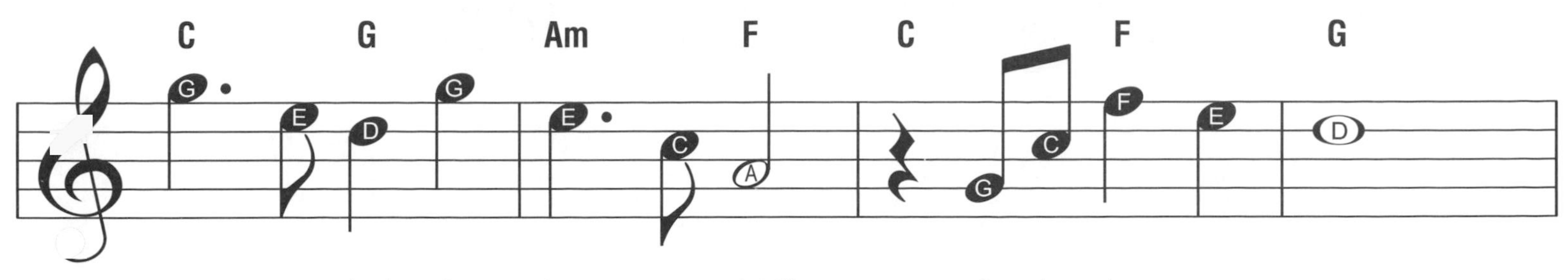
C G Am F C F G
can you feel the love to - night? It is where we are.

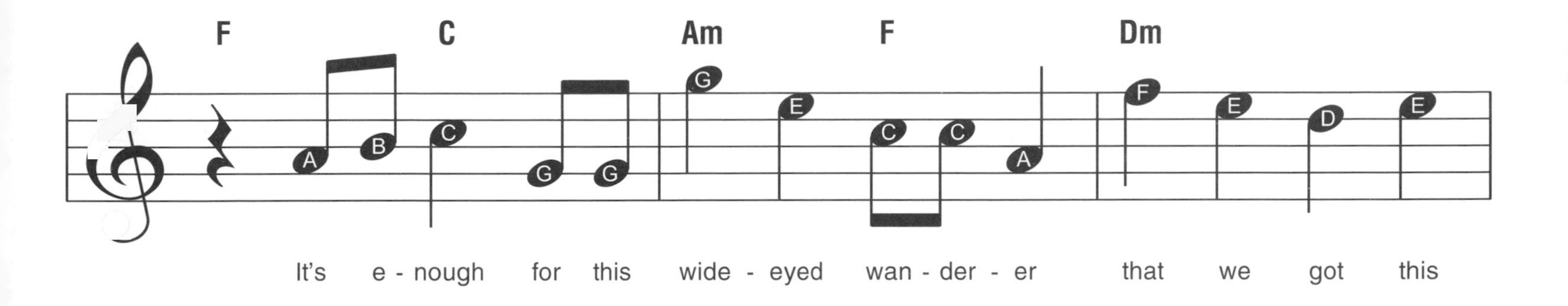
F C Am F Dm
It's e - nough for this wide - eyed wan - der - er that we got this

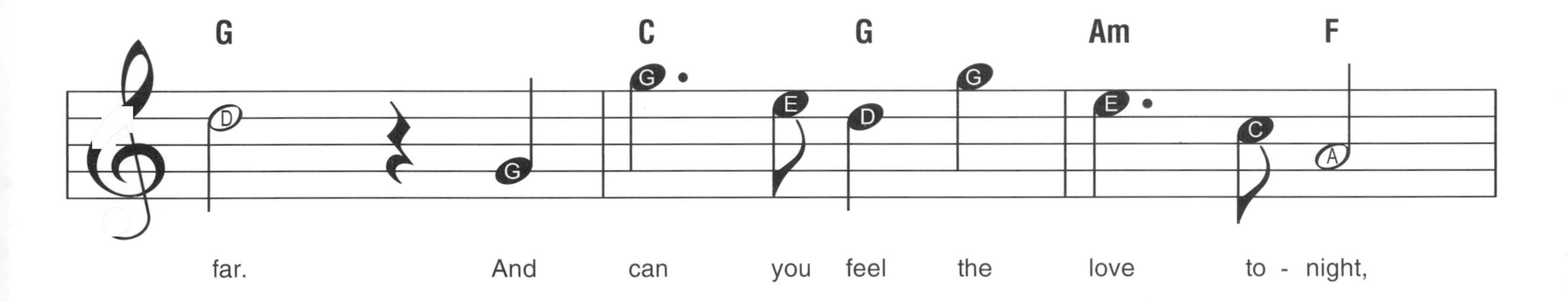
G C G Am F
far. And can you feel the love to - night,

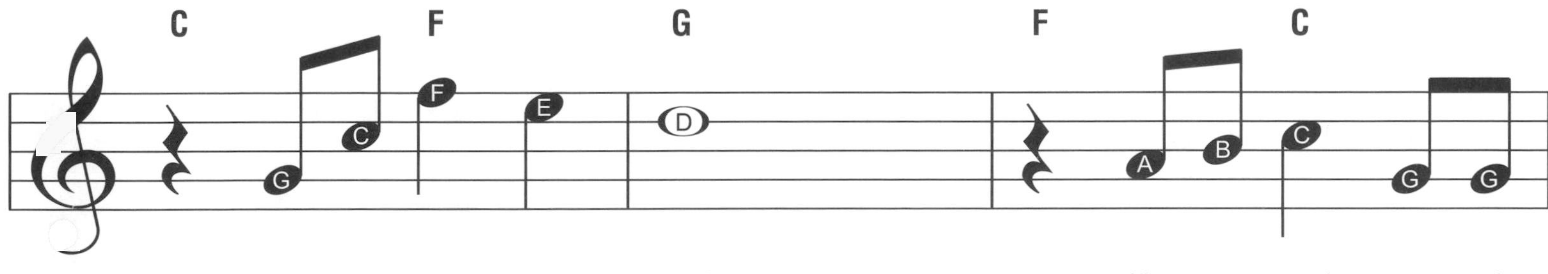
C F G F C
how it's laid to rest? It's e - nough to make

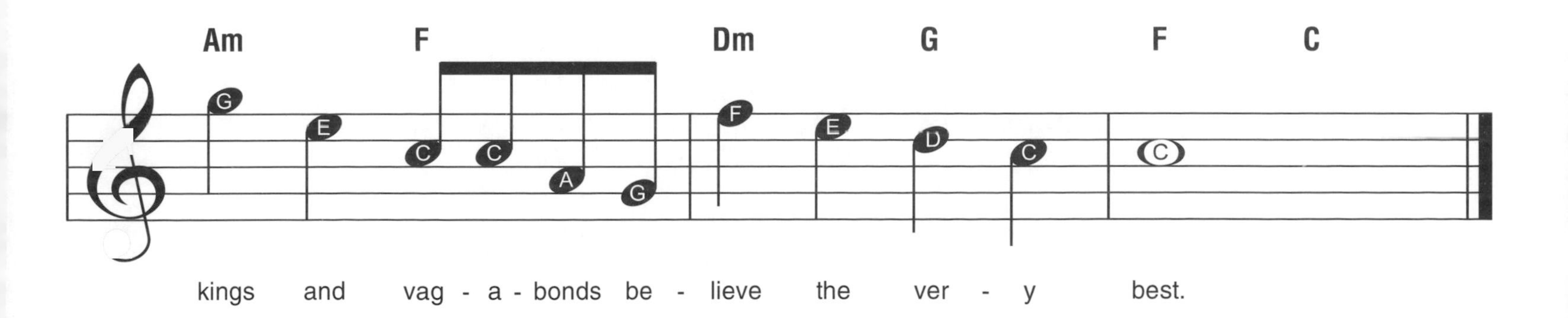
Am F Dm G F C
kings and vag - a - bonds be - lieve the ver - y best.

Candle in the Wind

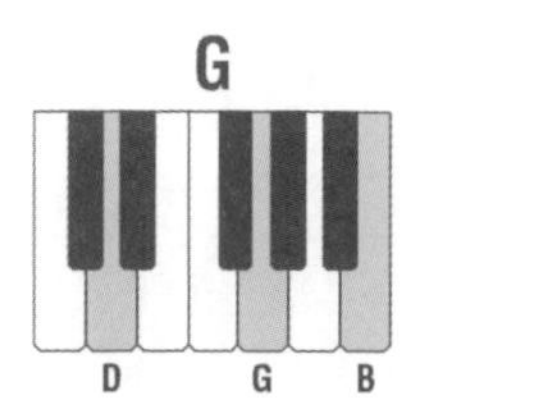

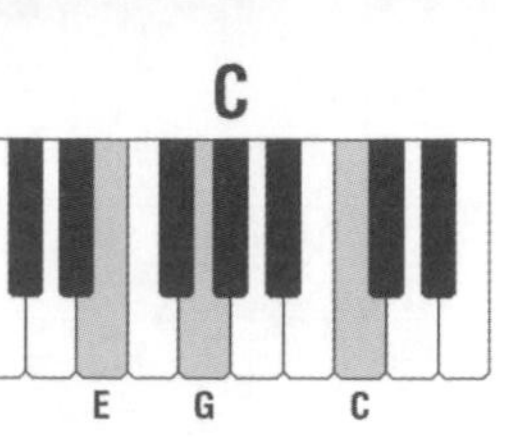

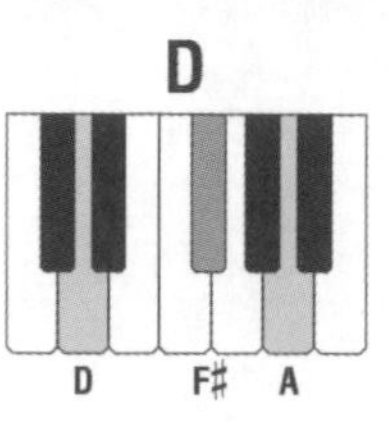

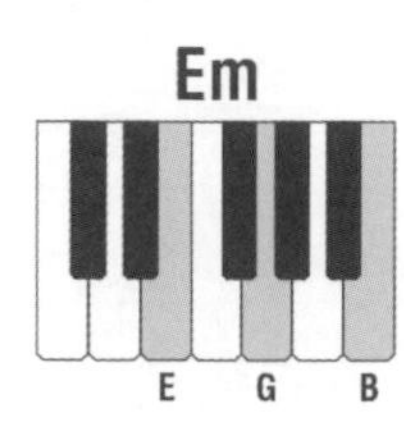

Words and Music by Elton John
and Bernie Taupin

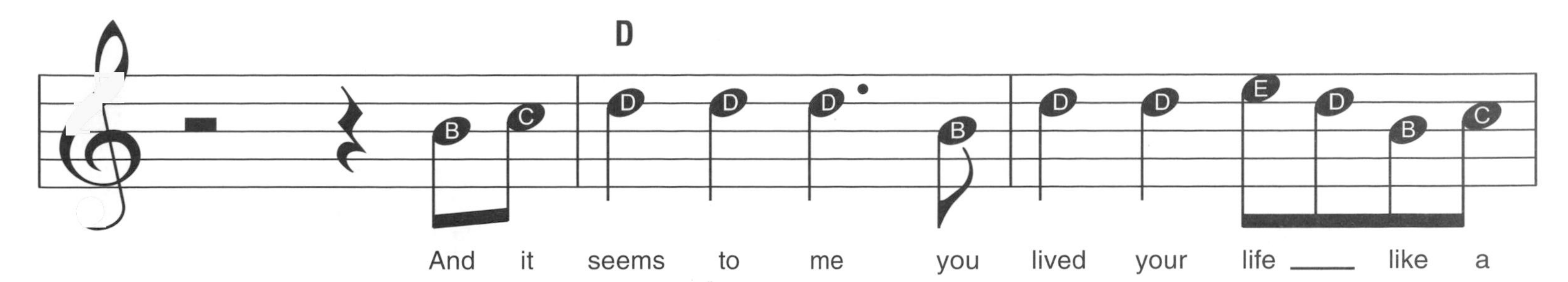
D
And it seems to me you lived your life ___ like a

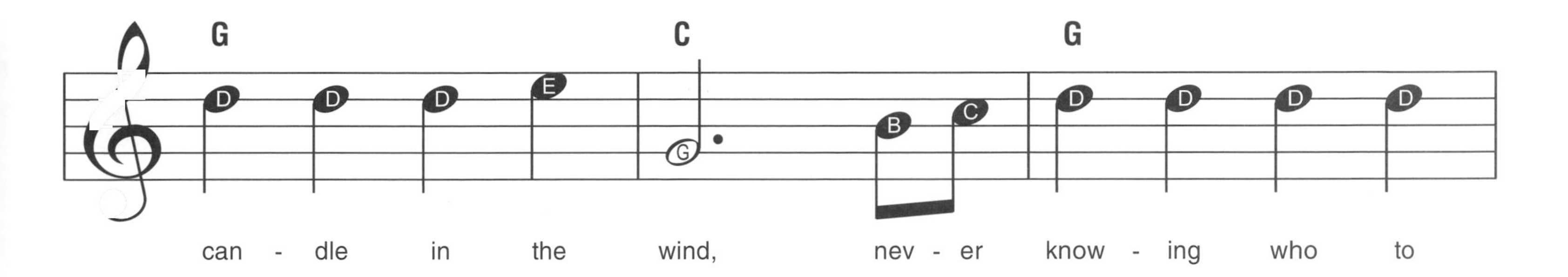
G
C
G
can - dle in the wind, nev - er know - ing who to

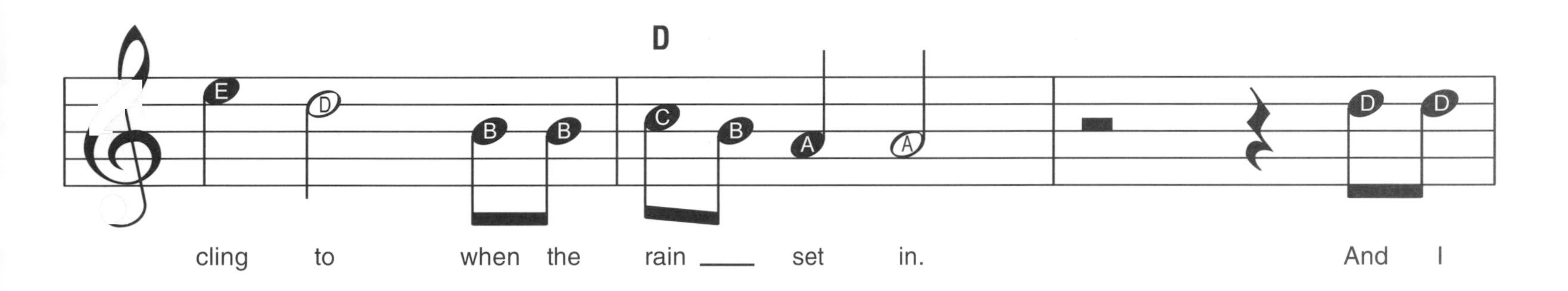
D
cling to when the rain ___ set in. And I

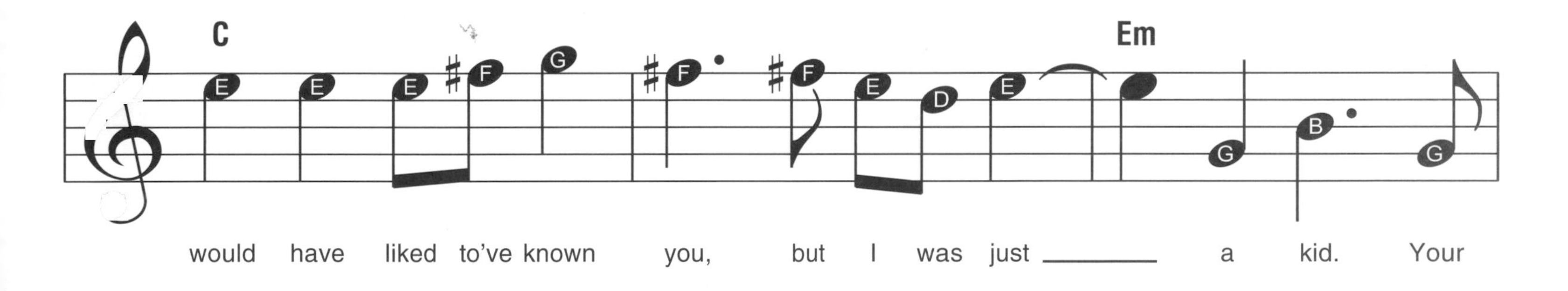
C
Em
would have liked to've known you, but I was just ___ a kid. Your

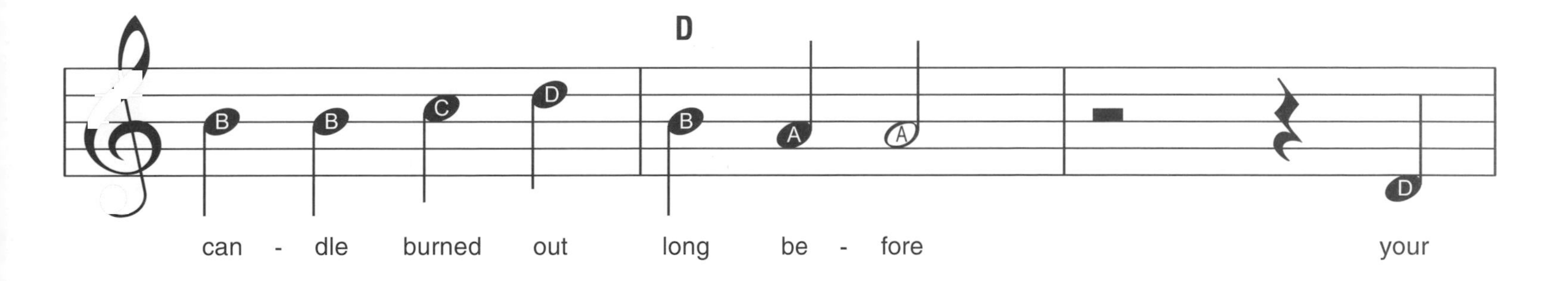
D
can - dle burned out long be - fore your

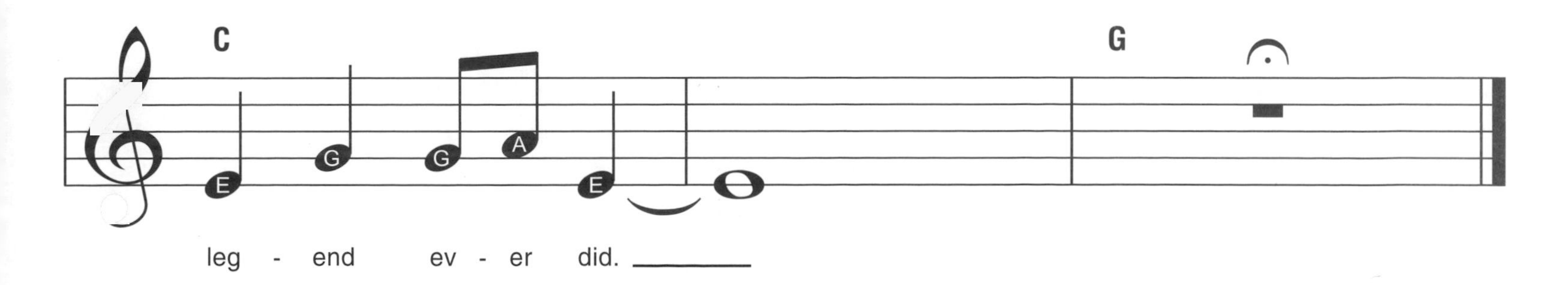
C
G
leg - end ev - er did. ___

Circle of Life

from THE LION KING

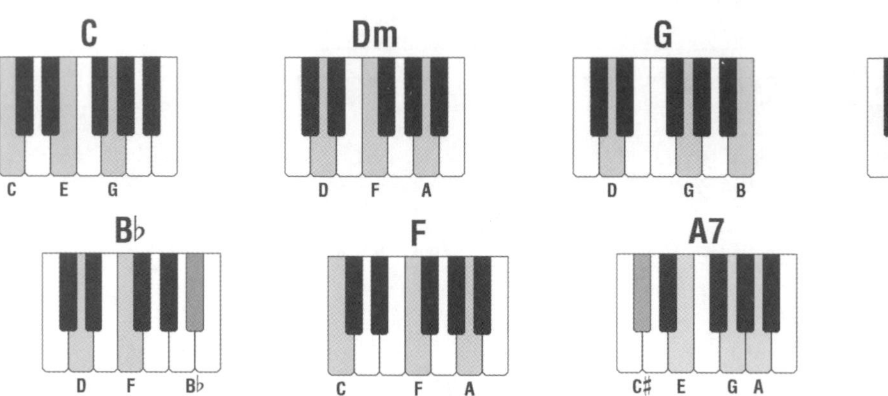

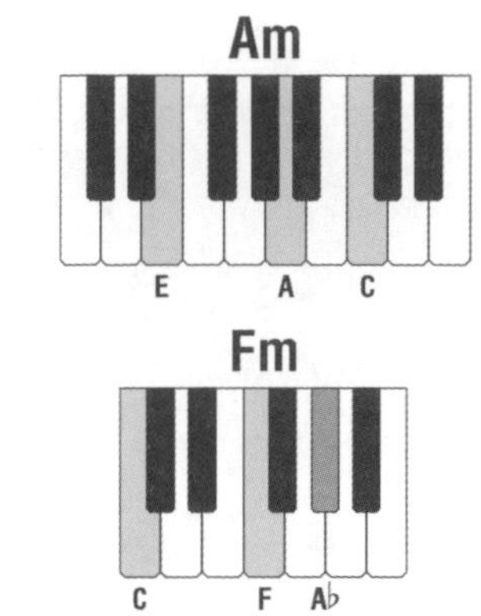

Music by Elton John
Lyrics by Tim Rice

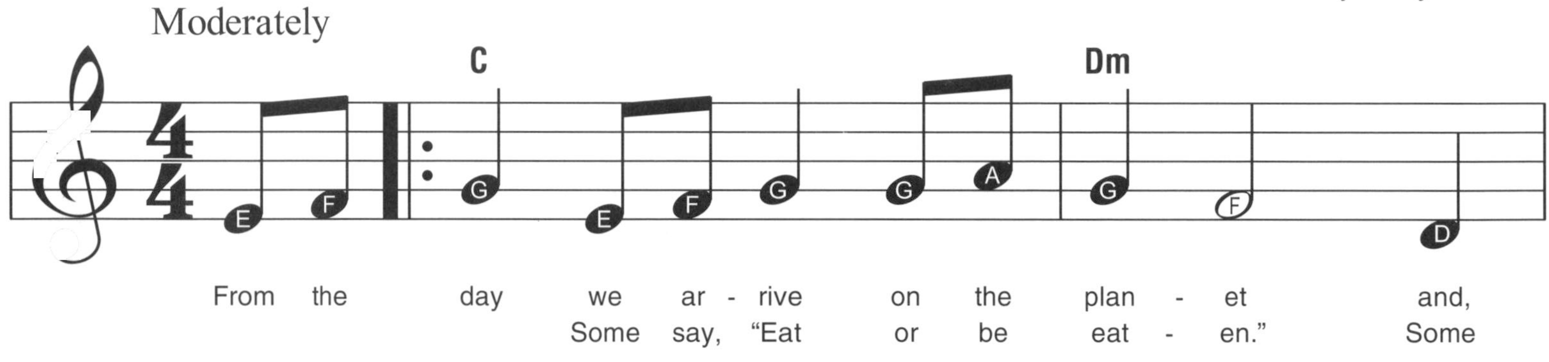

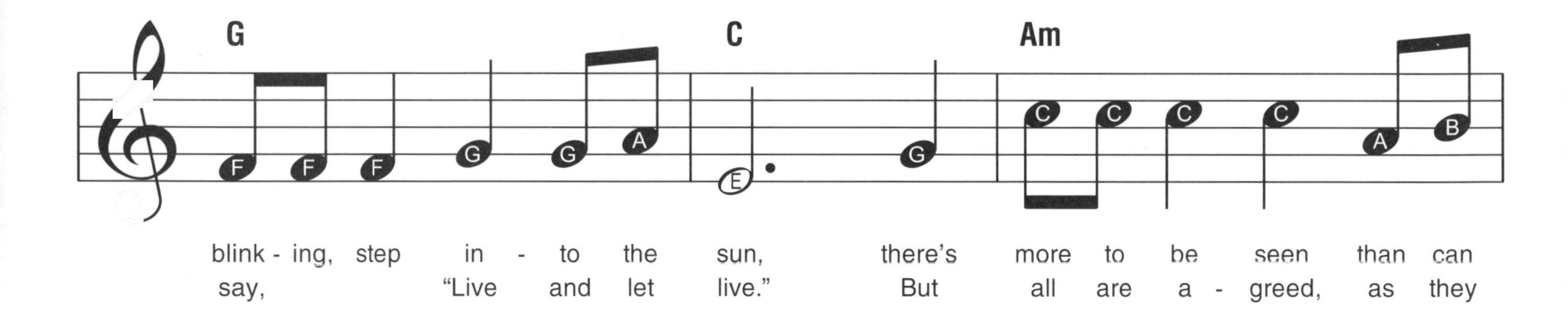

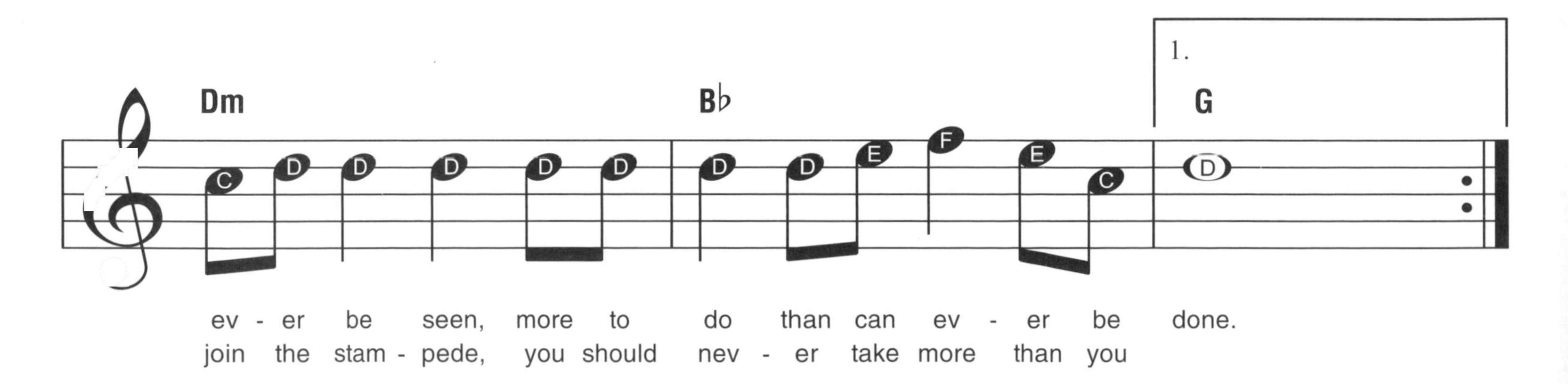

2.
G
C
give in the cir - cle of life.
It's the wheel of
B♭
F
for - tune,
it's the leap of faith,
G
it's the band of hope
till we find our
C
A7
place
on the path un -
Dm
Fm
C
wind - ing
in the cir - cle,
G
F
C
the cir - cle of life.

Crocodile Rock

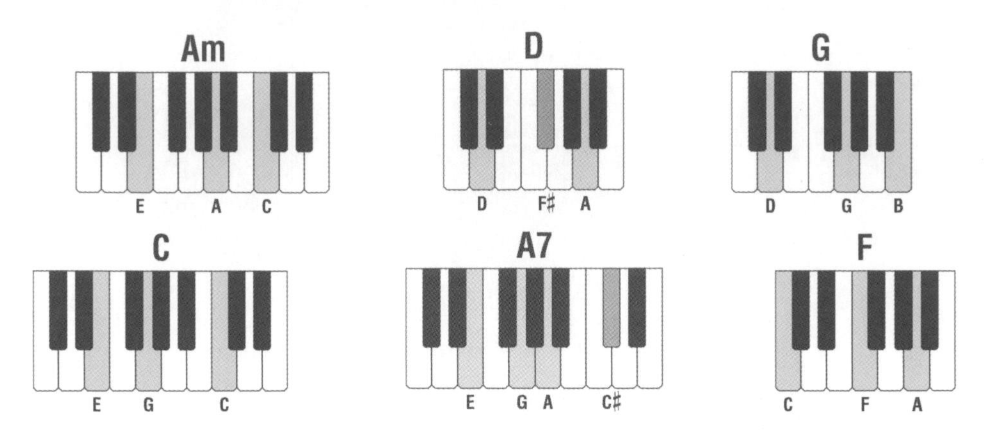

Words and Music by Elton John
and Bernie Taupin

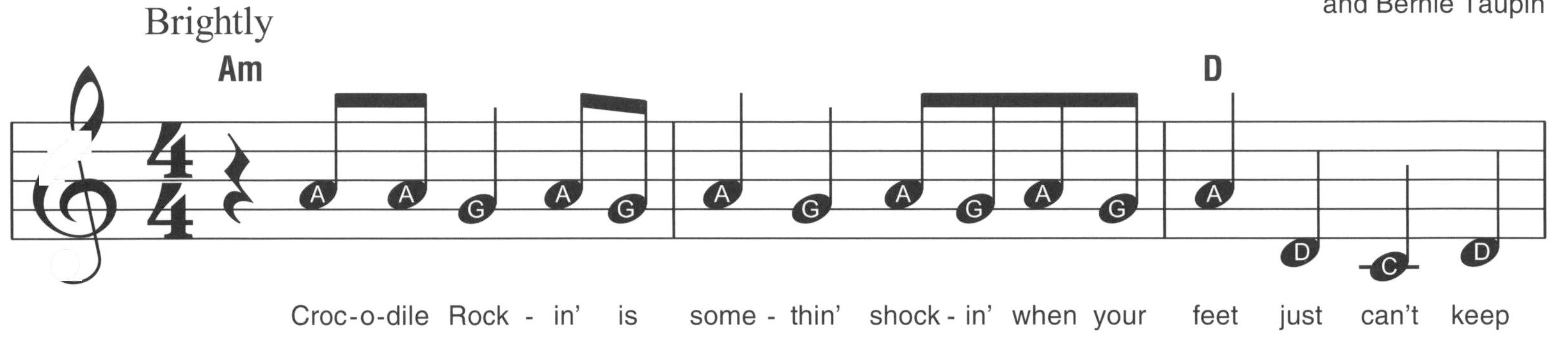

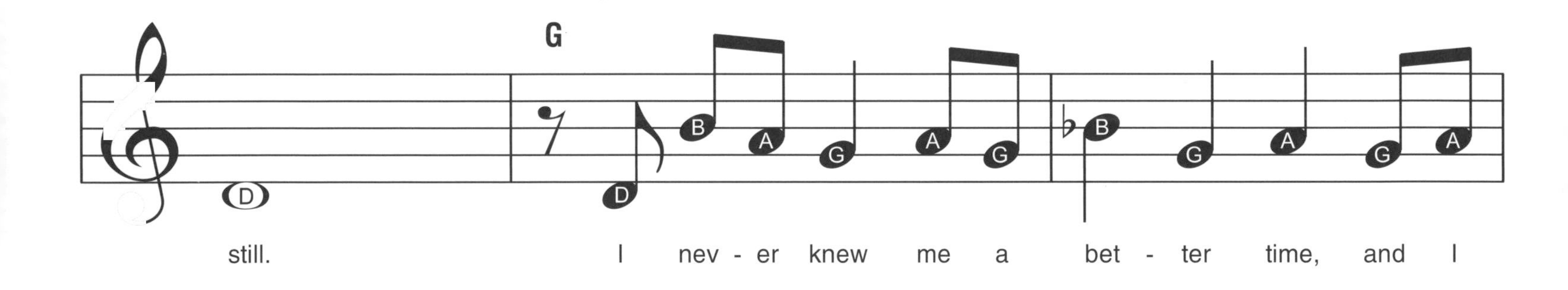

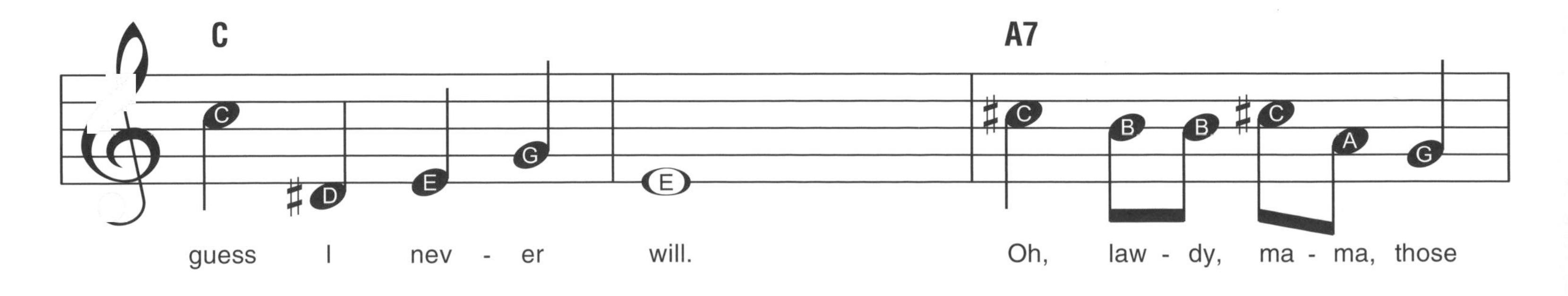

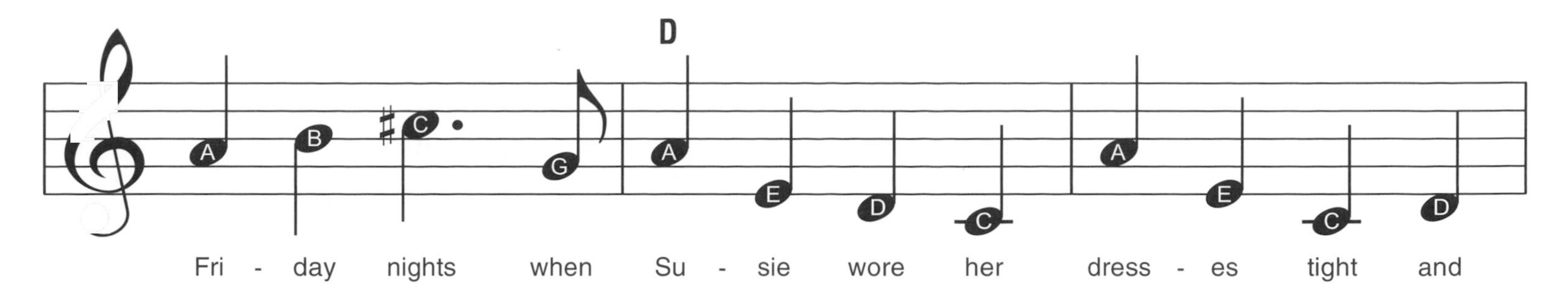
D
Fri - day nights when Su - sie wore her dress - es tight and

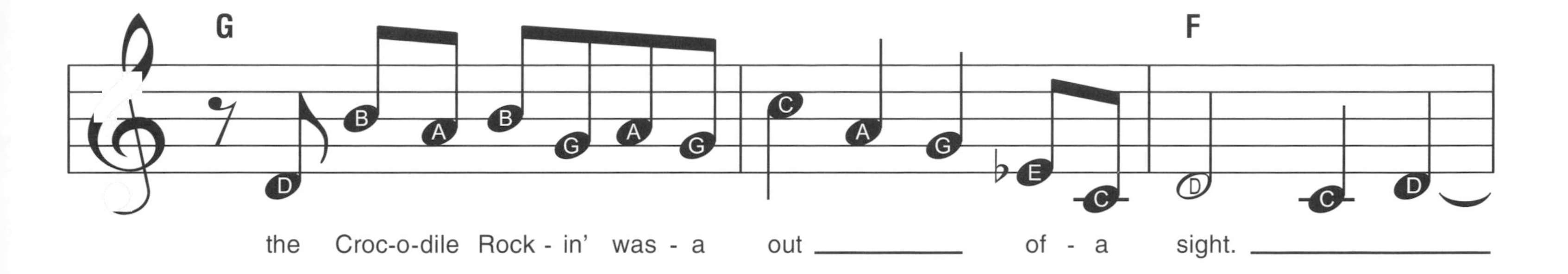
G
F
the Croc-o-dile Rock - in' was - a out of - a sight.

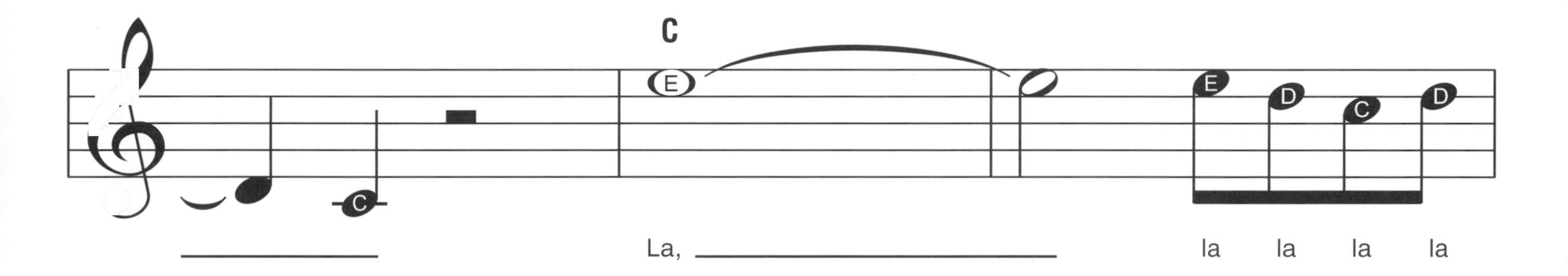
C
La, la la la la

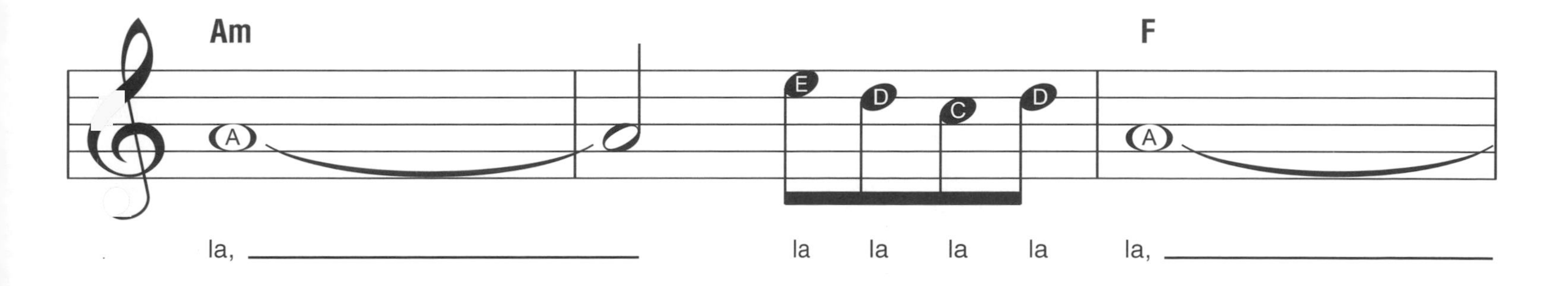
Am
F
la, la la la la la,

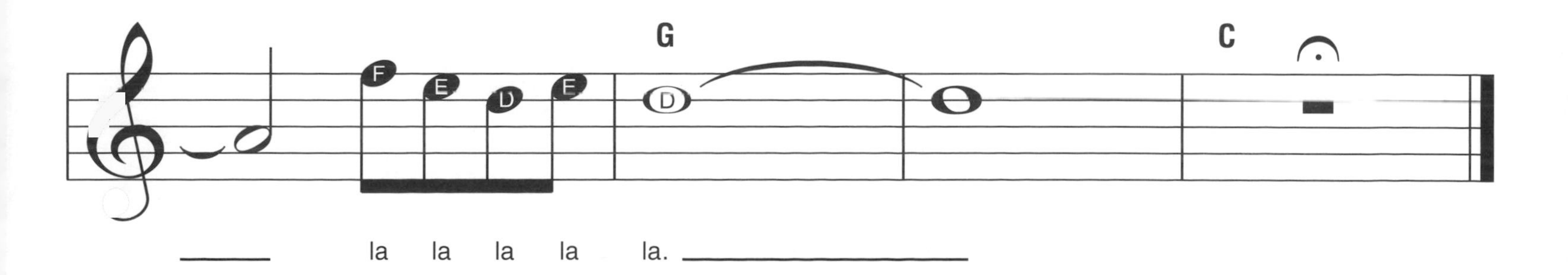
G
C
la la la la la.

Daniel

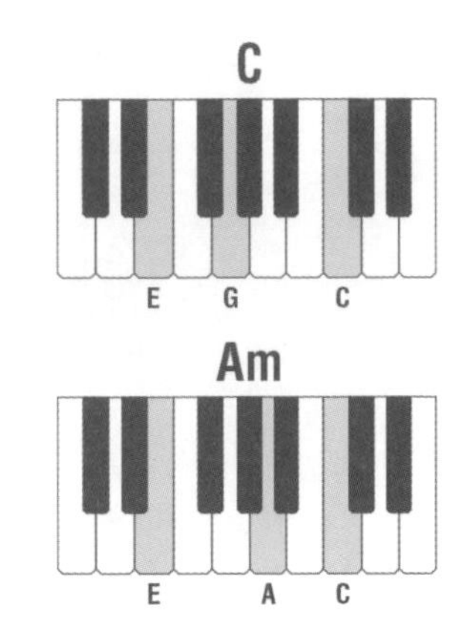

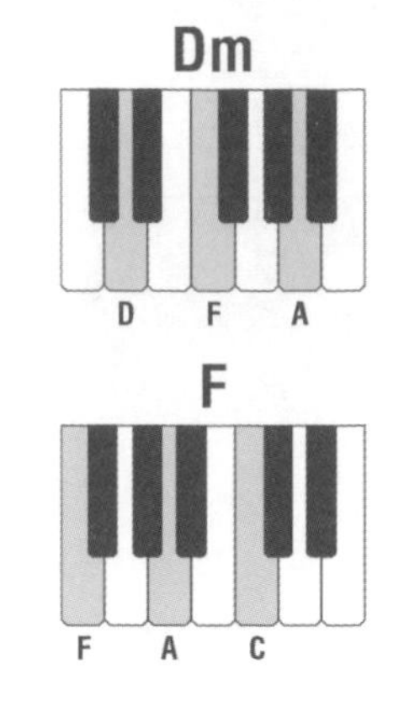

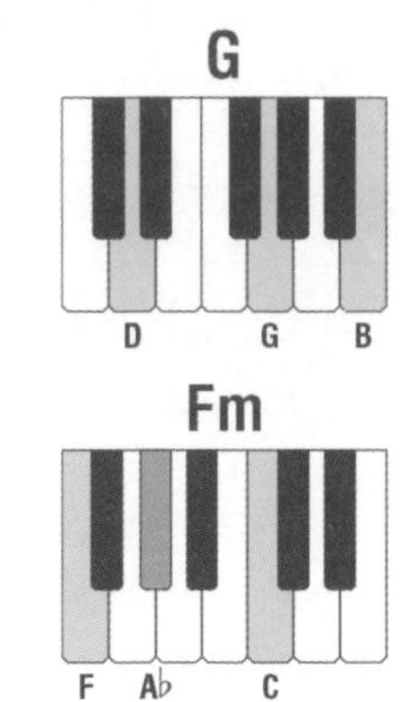

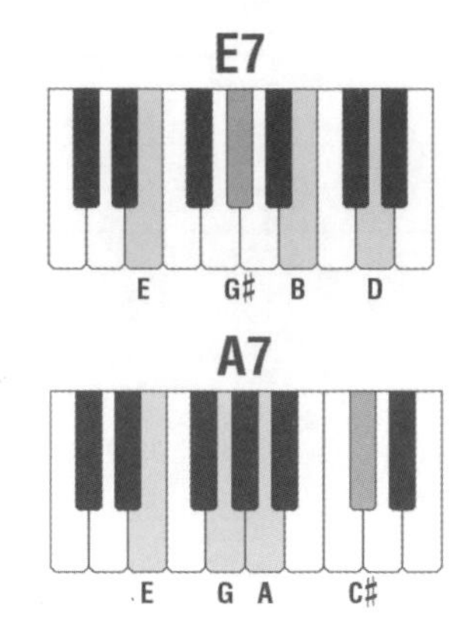

Words and Music by Elton John
and Bernie Taupin

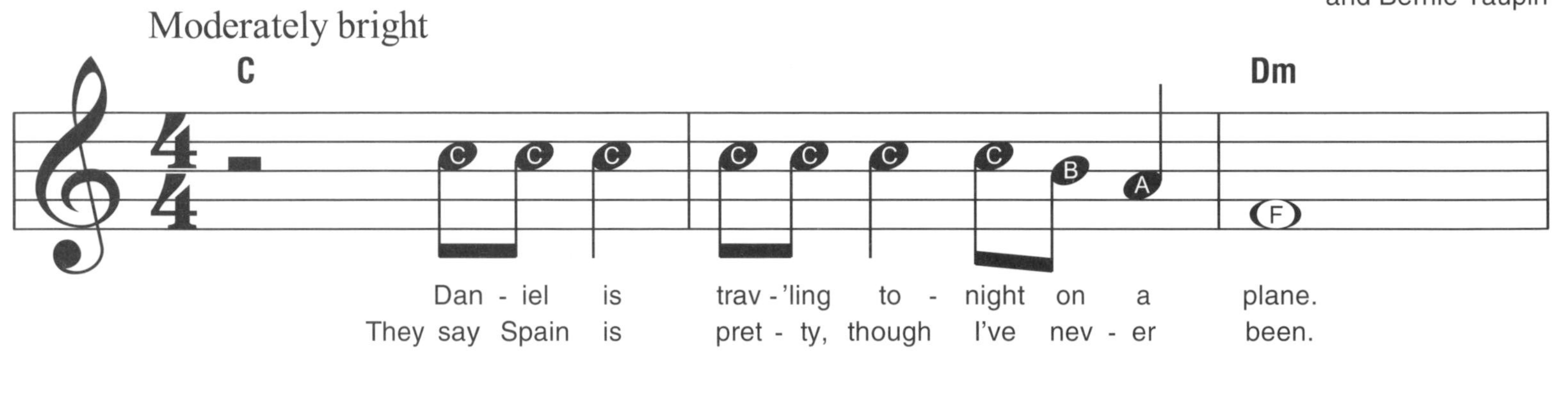

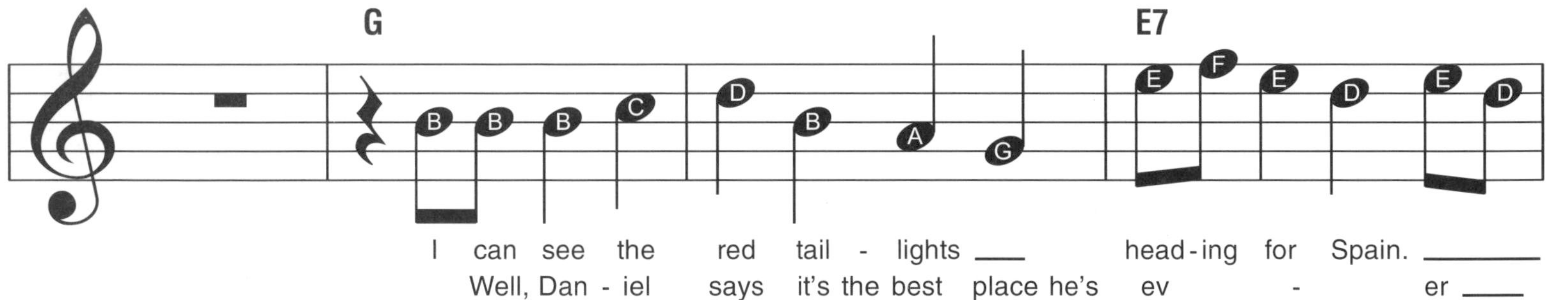

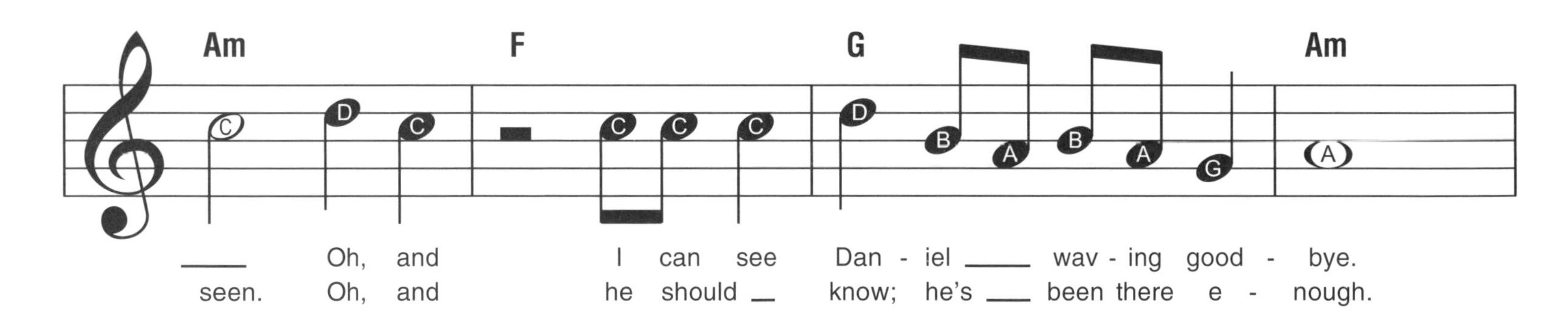

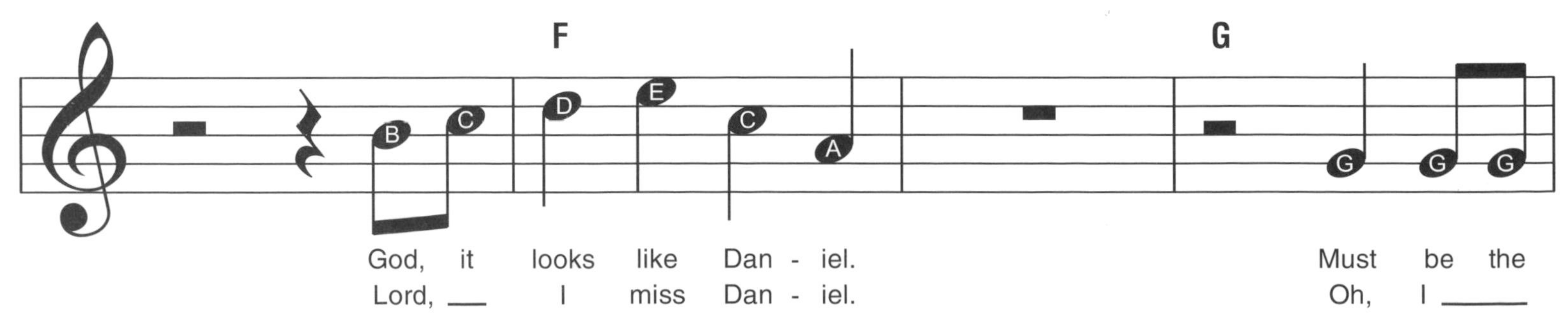

1.
C
G
clouds in my eyes.
miss him so
(Instrumental)
2.
C
F
much.
Oh,
Dan - iel, my
C
F
broth - er, you are old - er than me. Do you still feel the pain
C
Am
of the scars that won't heal? Your eyes have died, but
F
Fm
C
you see more than I.
Dan - iel, you're a star
A7
Dm
G
C
in the face of the sky.

Don't Go Breaking My Heart

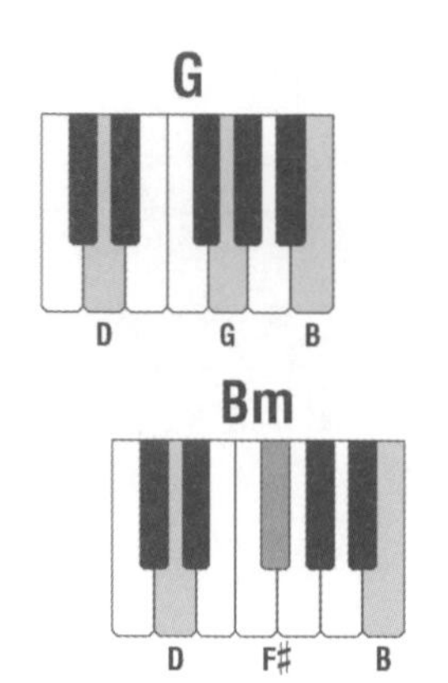

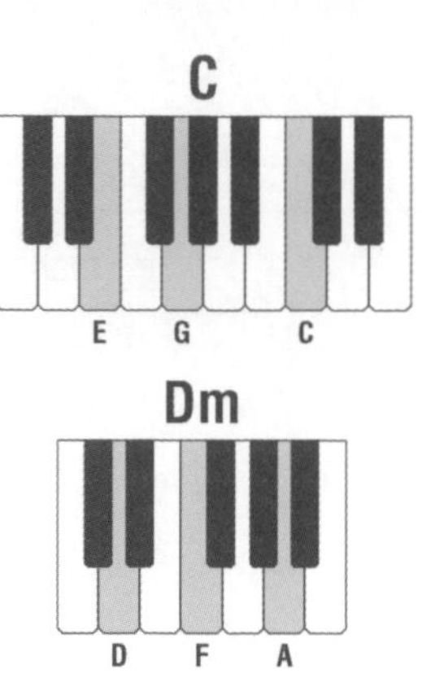

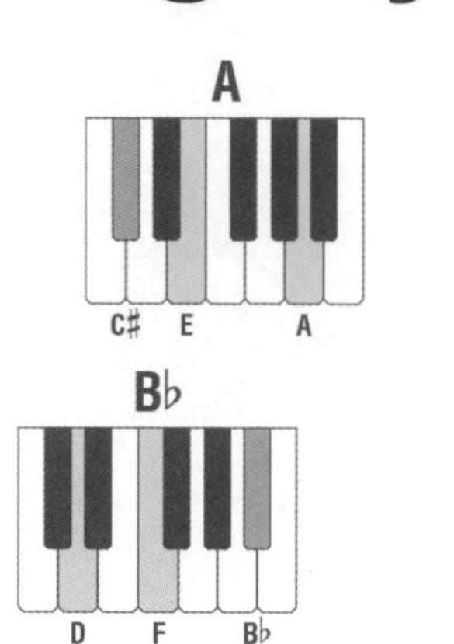

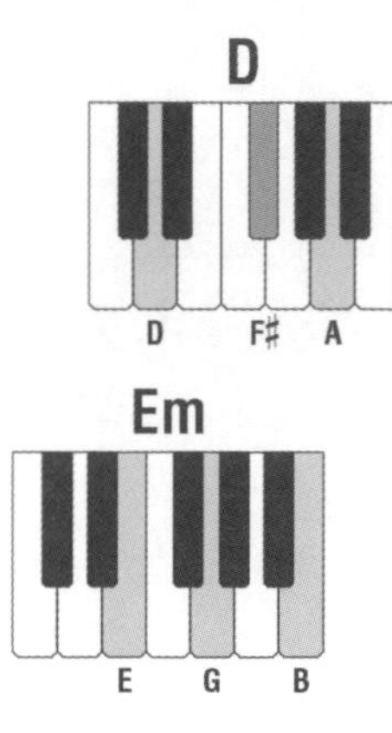

Words and Music by Carte Blanche
and Ann Orson

Moderately fast

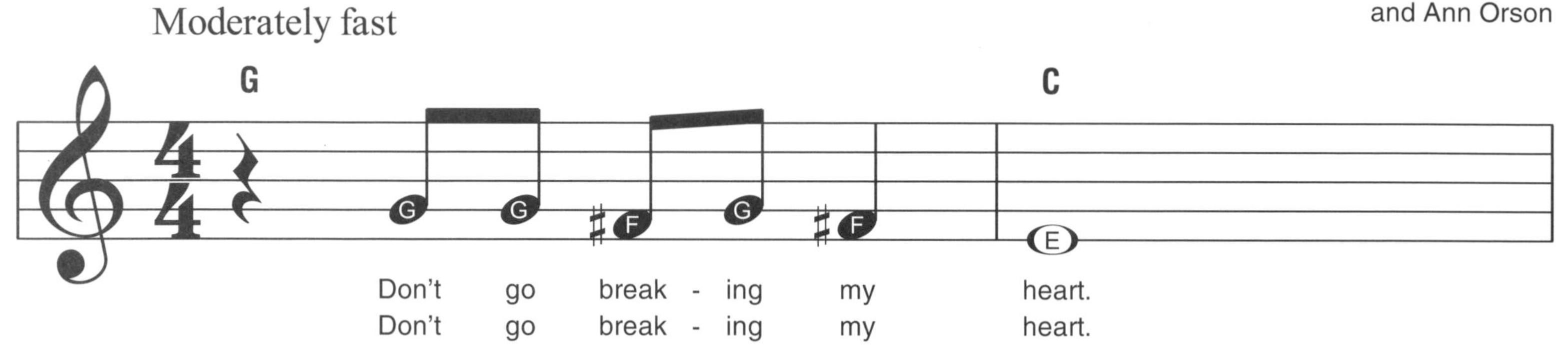

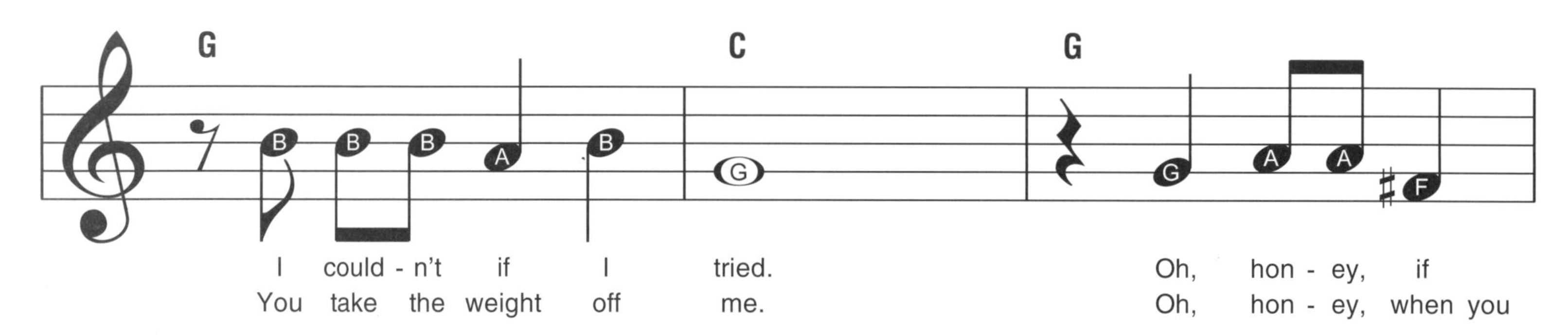

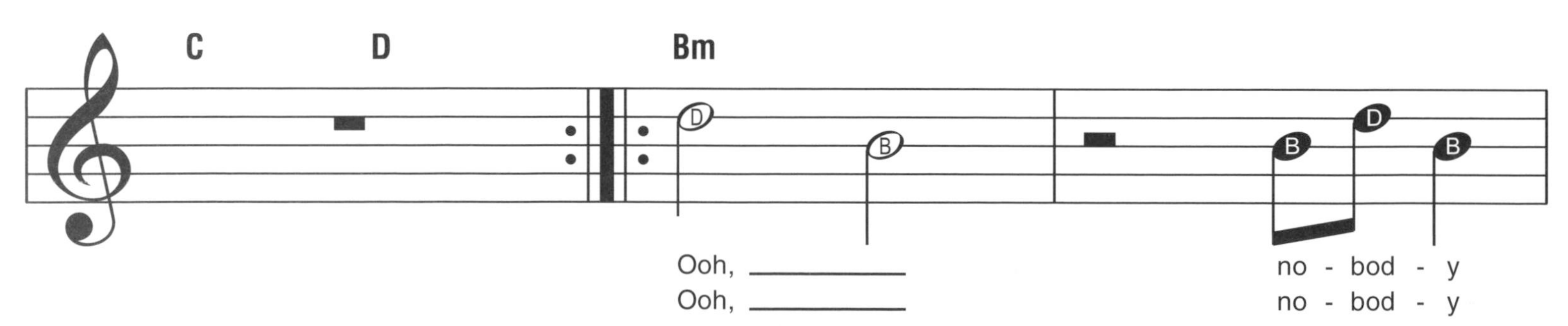

Dm C G
knows it, but when I was down,
knows it, but right from the start, I
D A B♭ D
I was your clown. Oh, I gave you my
gave you my heart.
C G C D G
heart. So, don't go break - ing my
Em C D G
heart. I won't go break - ing your heart.
Em C D G
Don't go break - ing my heart.

Don't Let the Sun Go Down on Me

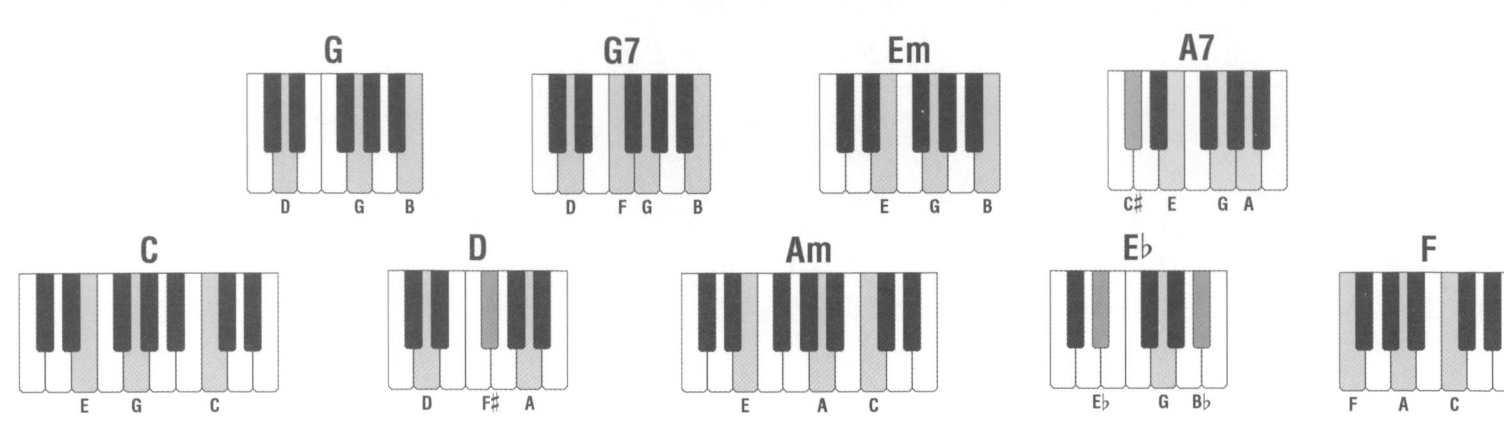

Words and Music by Elton John
and Bernie Taupin

Moderately slow, in 2

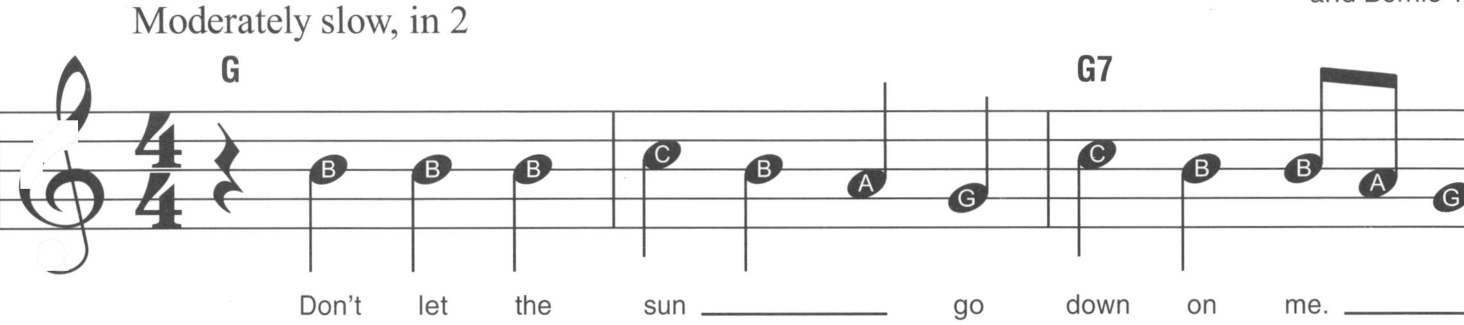

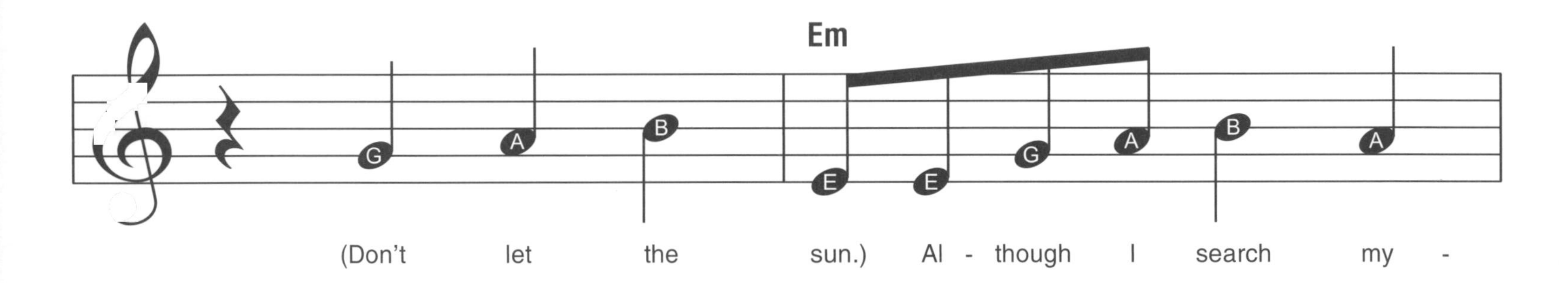

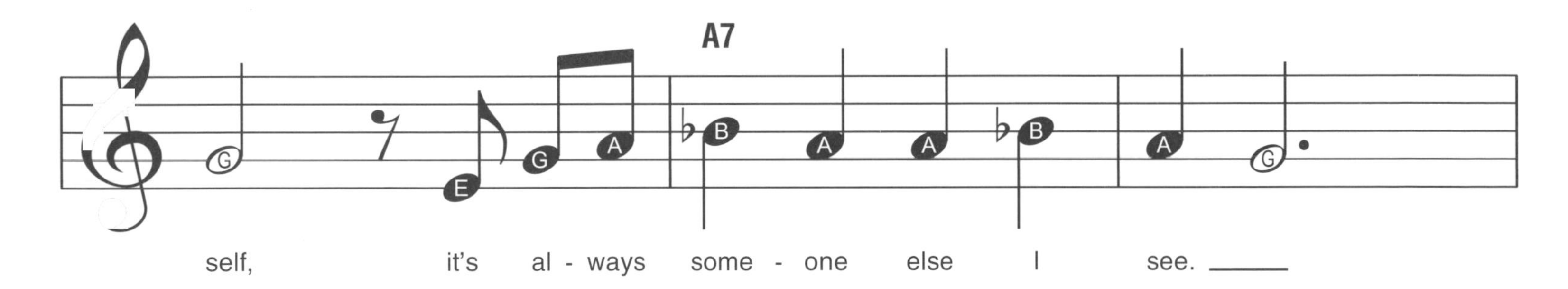

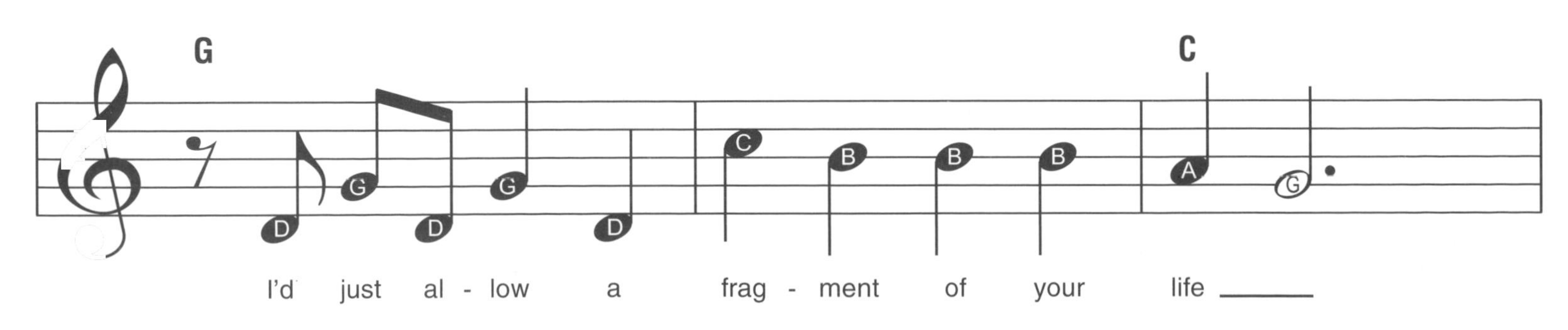

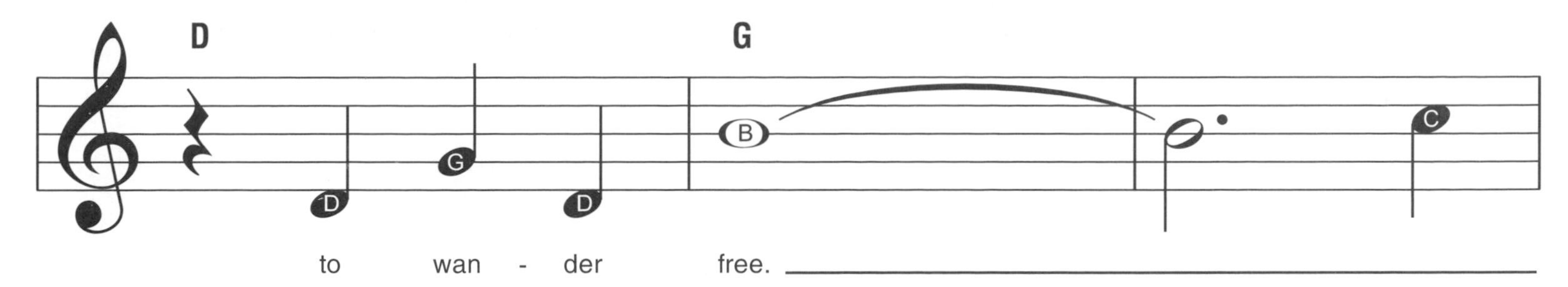
D
G
to wan - der free.

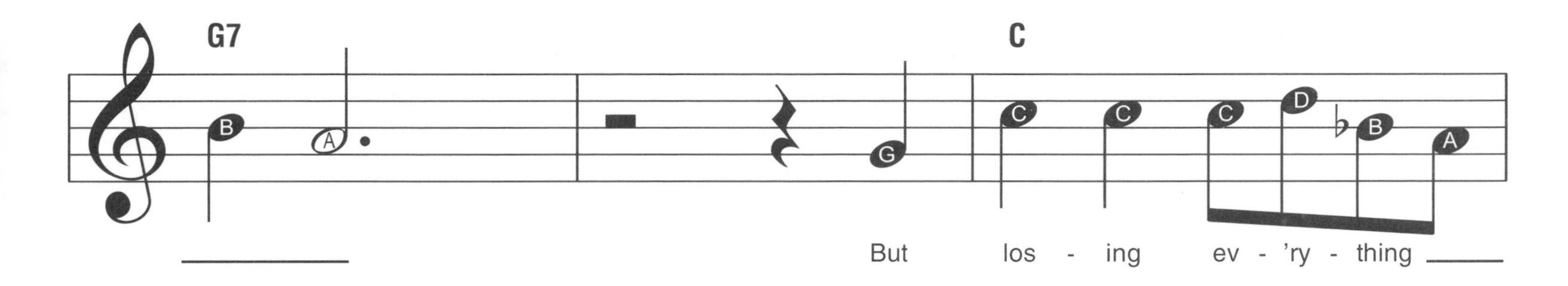
G7
C
But los - ing ev - 'ry - thing

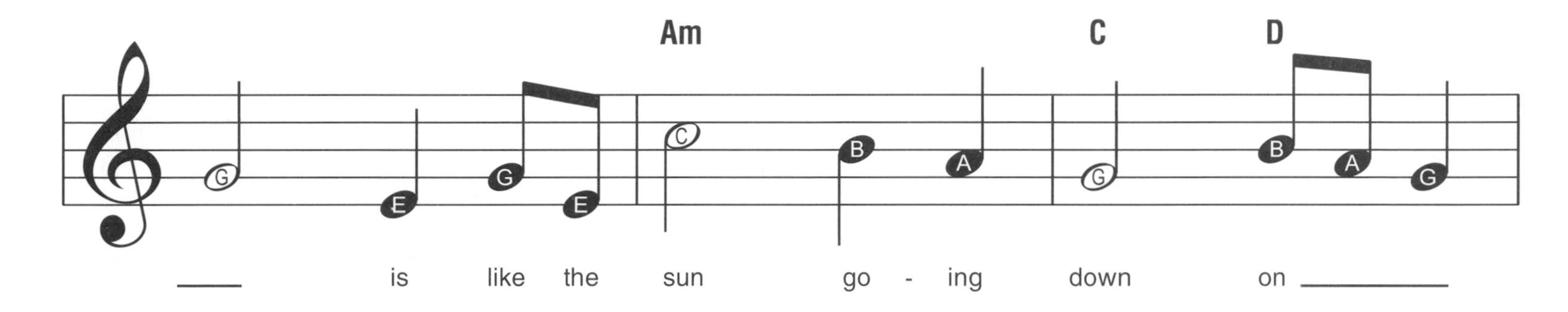
Am
C
D
is like the sun go - ing down on

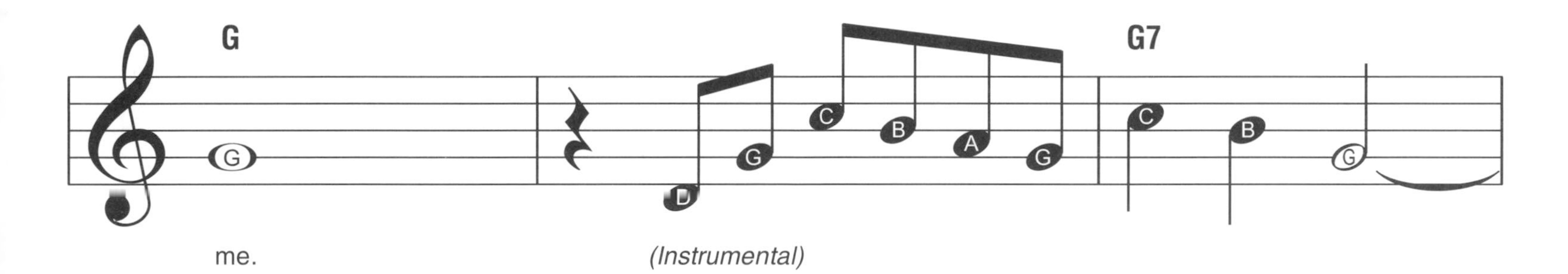
G
G7
me.
(Instrumental)

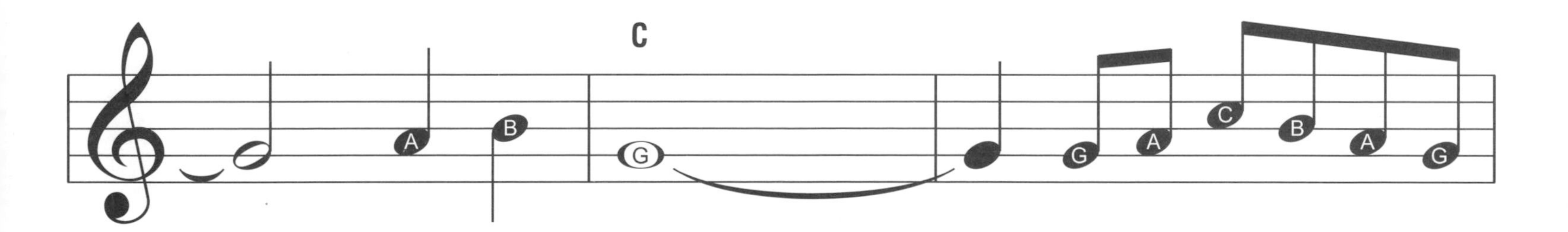
C

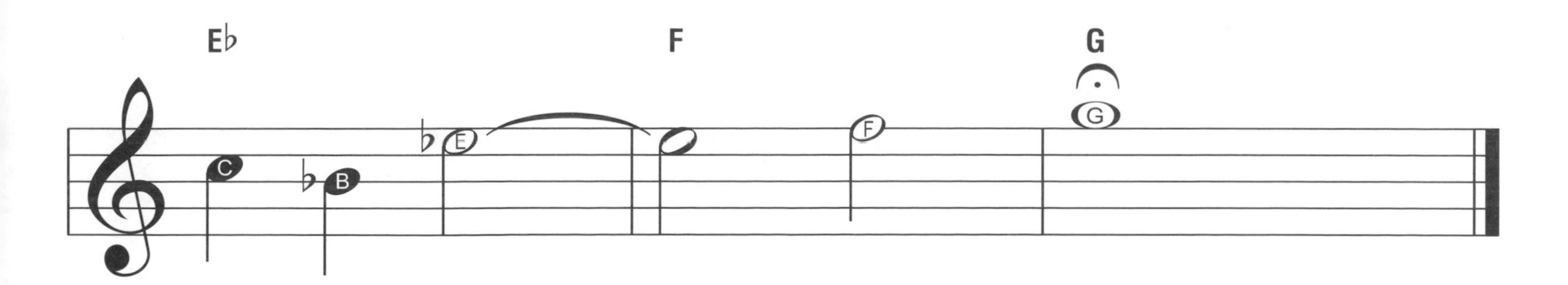
E♭
F
G

Goodbye Yellow Brick Road

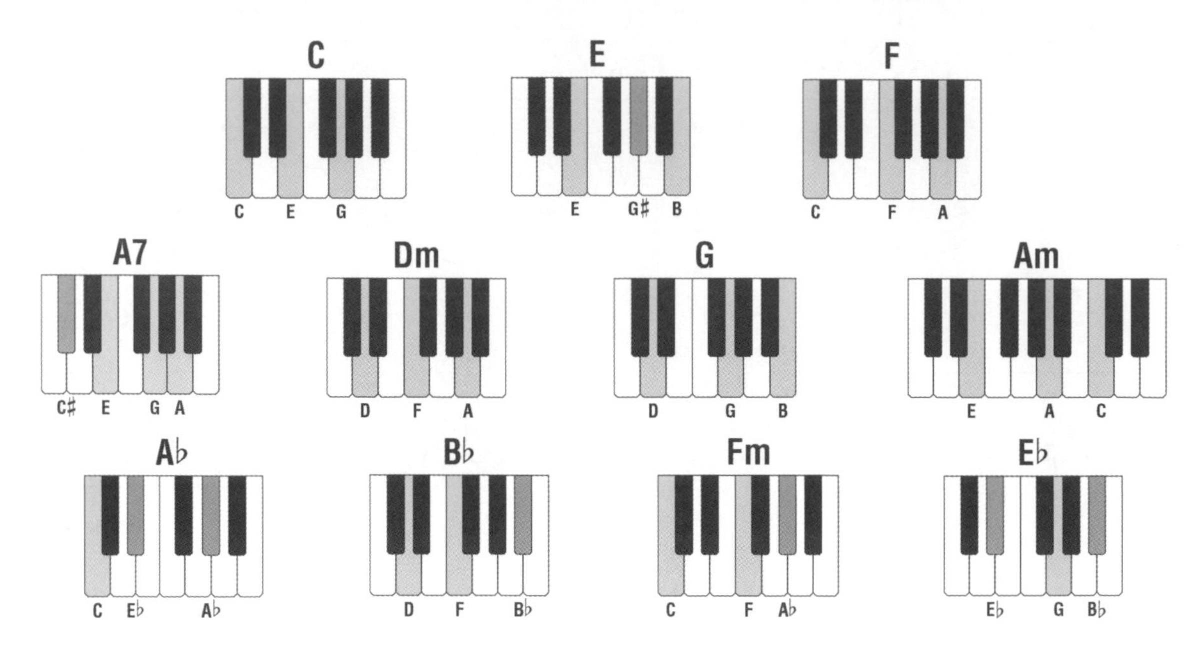

Words and Music by Elton John
and Bernie Taupin

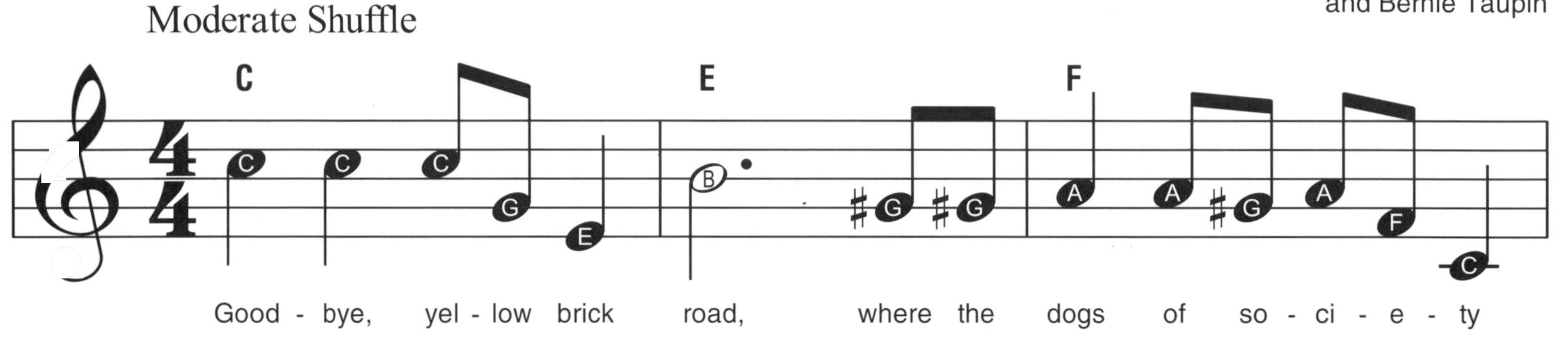

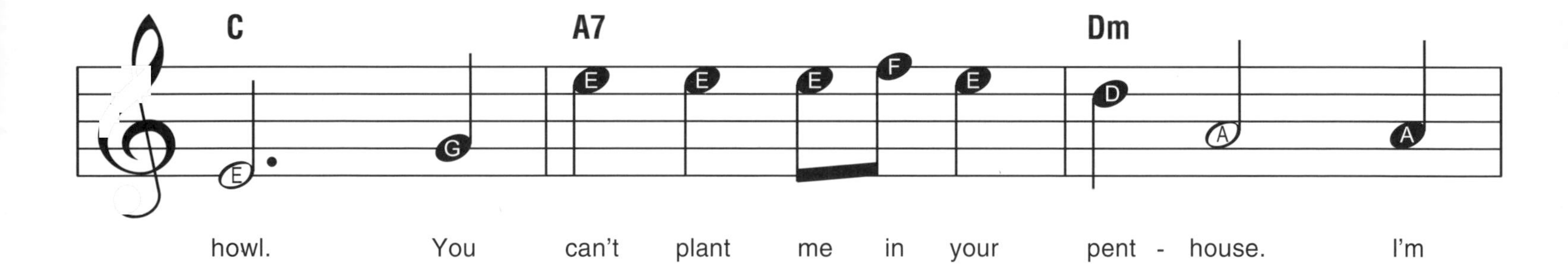

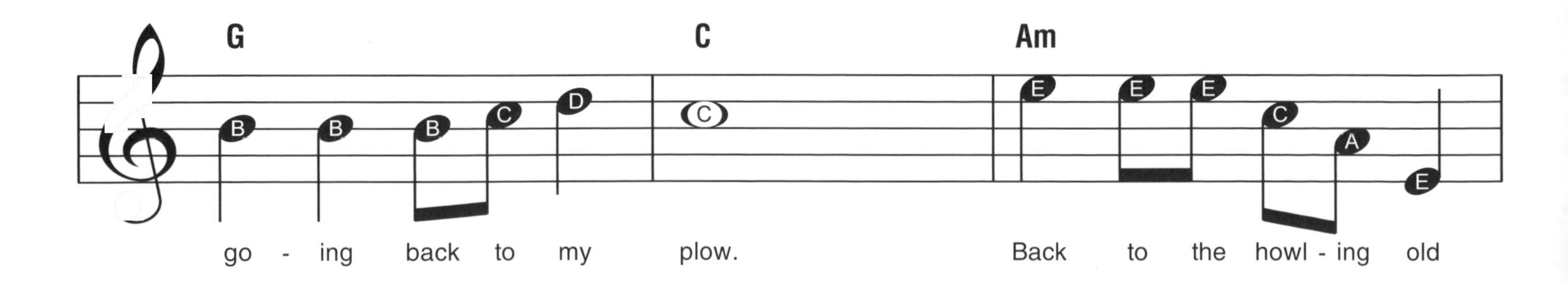

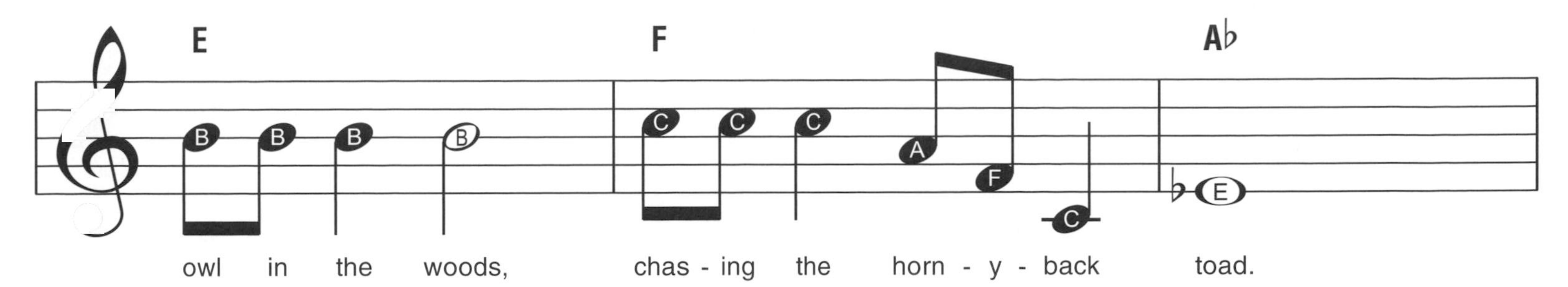
E
F
A♭
B B B B
C C C A F C
E
owl in the woods,
chas - ing the horn - y - back toad.

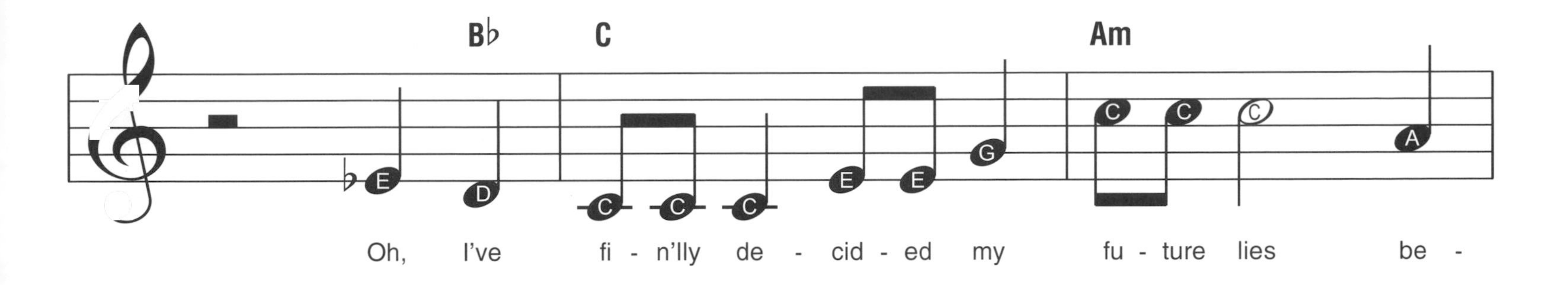
B♭
C
Am
E D
C C C E E G
C C C A
Oh, I've
fi - n'lly de - cid - ed my
fu - ture lies be -

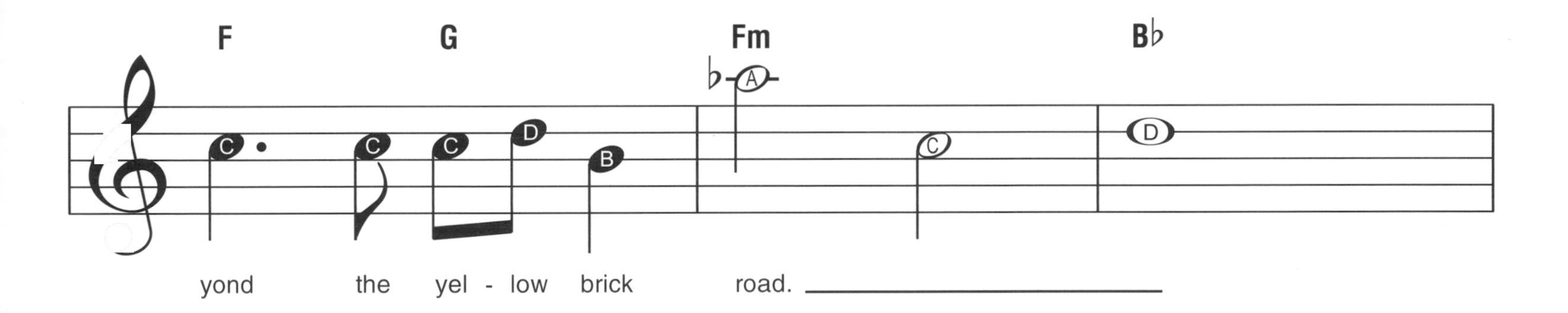
F
G
Fm
B♭
C C C D B
A C
D
yond the yel - low brick road.

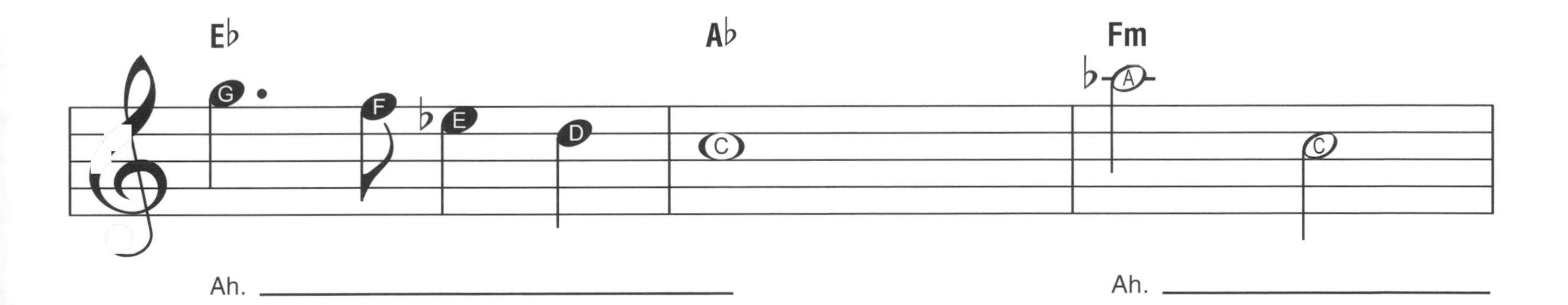
E♭
A♭
Fm
G F E D
C
A C
Ah.
Ah.

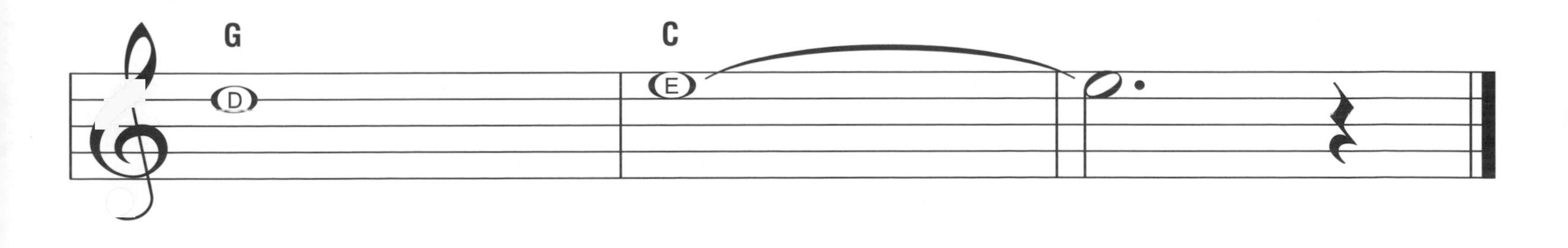
G
C
D
E

Honky Cat

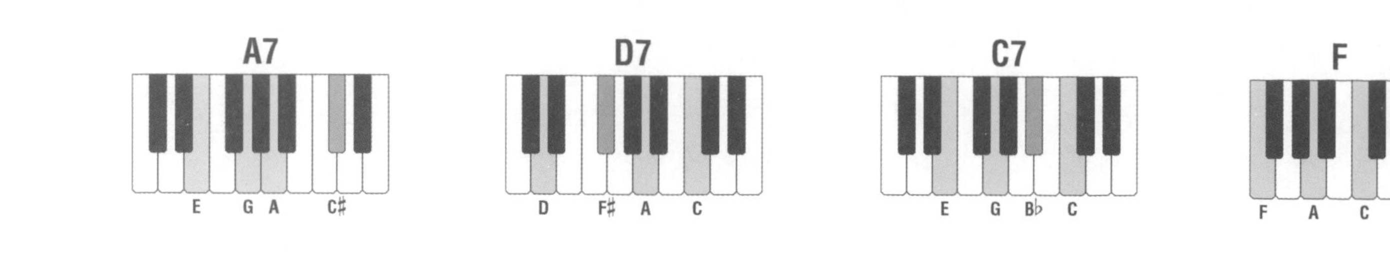

Words and Music by Elton John
and Bernie Taupin

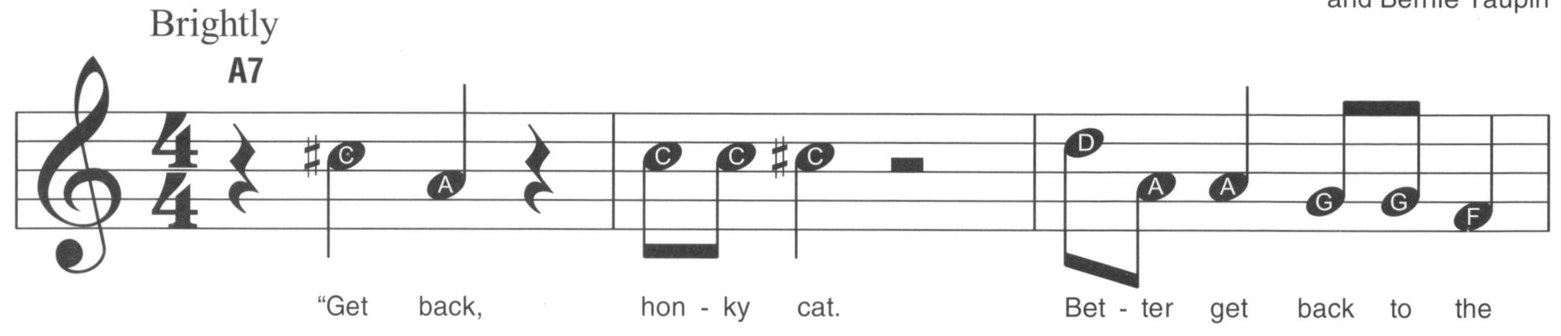

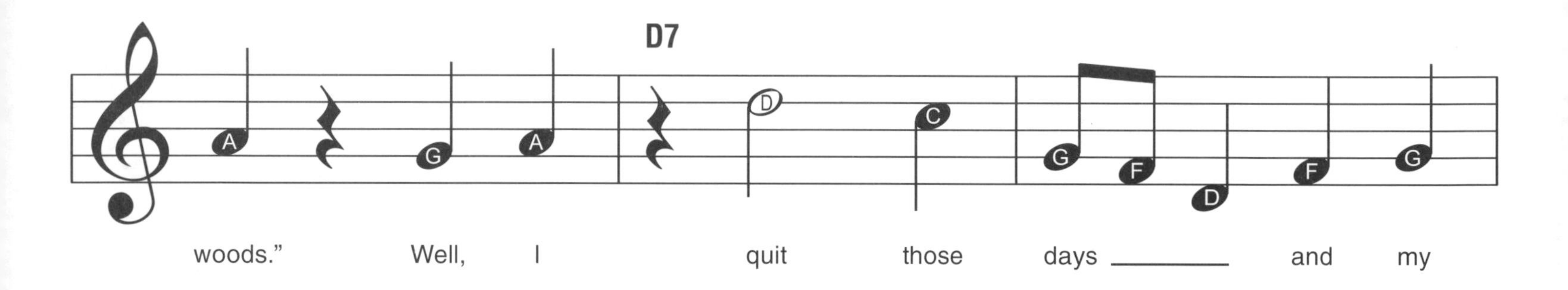

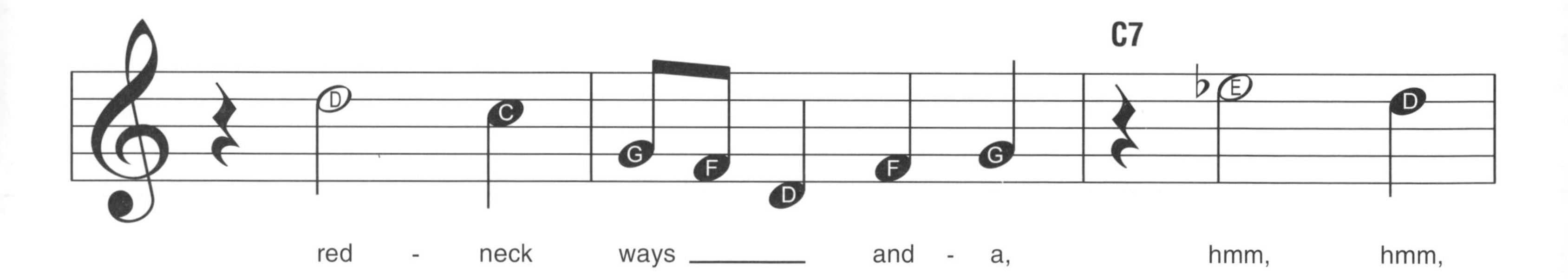

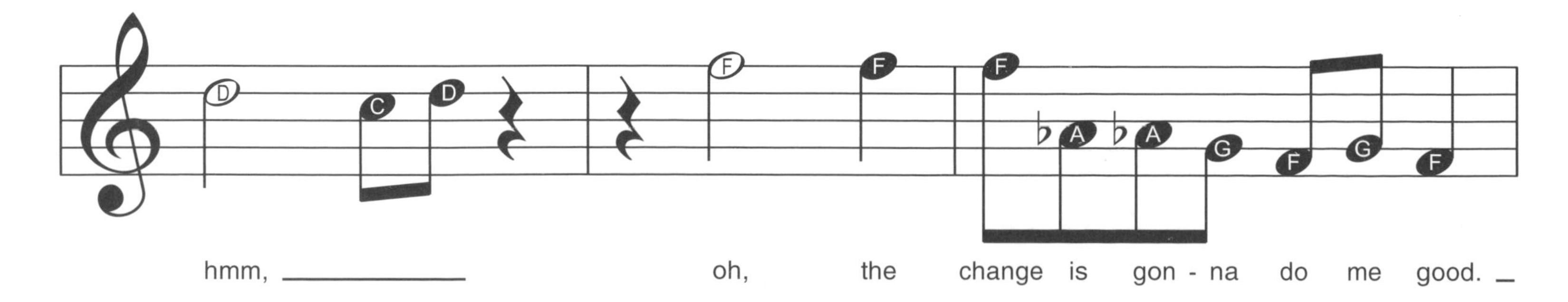

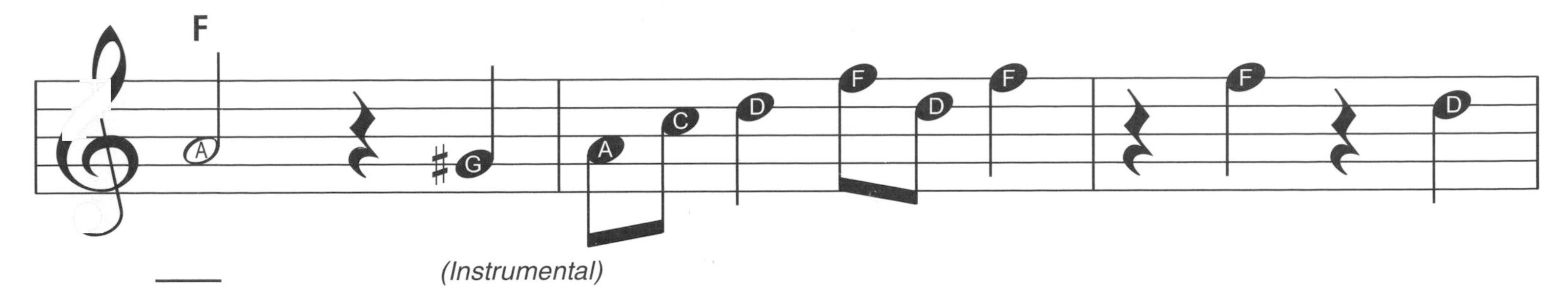
F
(Instrumental)

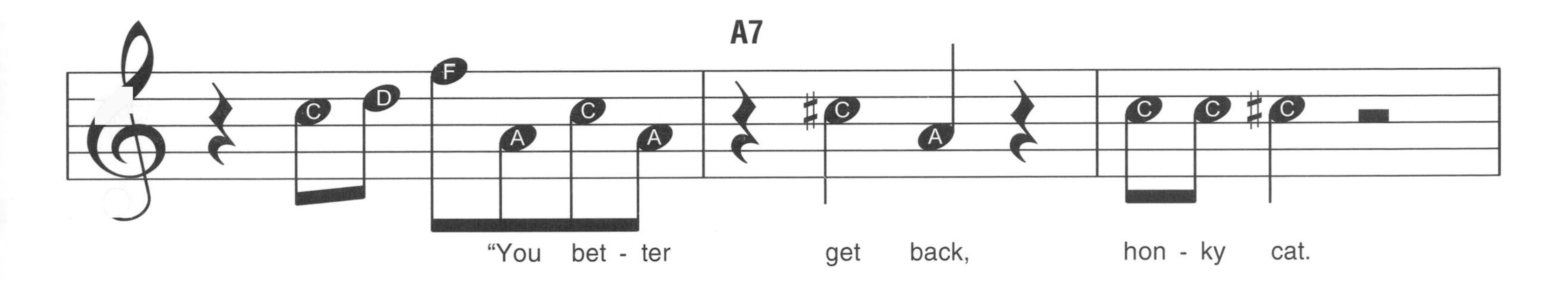
A7
"You bet - ter get back, hon - ky cat.

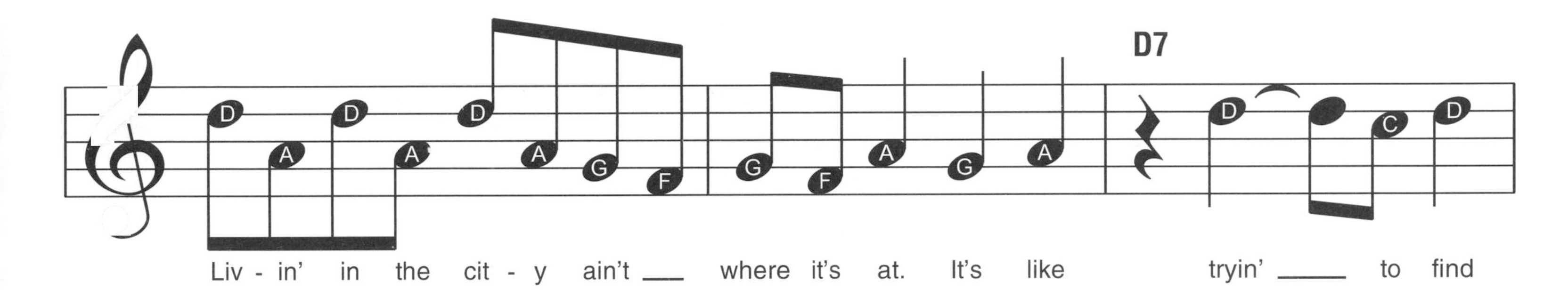
D7
Liv - in' in the cit - y ain't where it's at. It's like tryin' to find

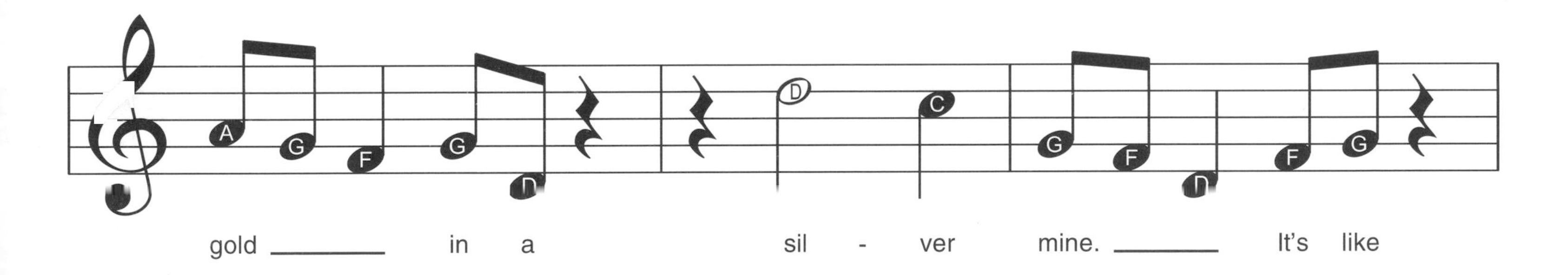
gold in a sil - ver mine. It's like

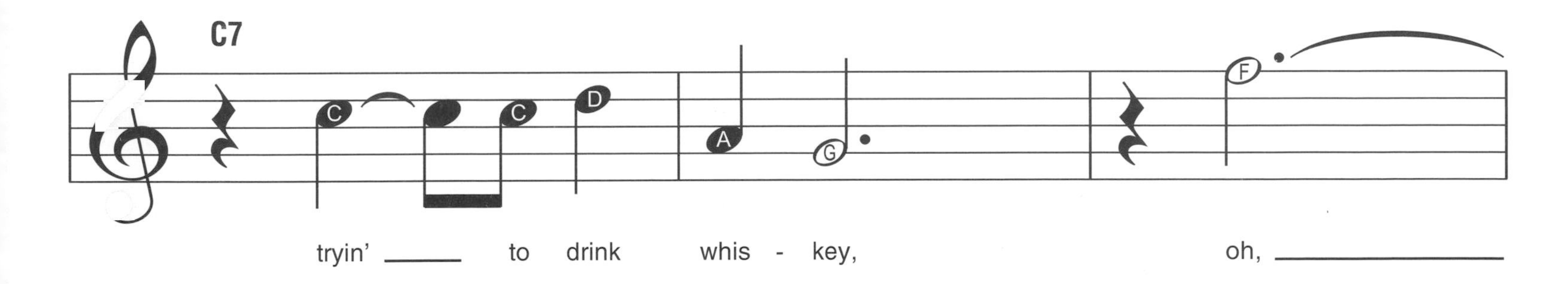
C7
tryin' to drink whis - key, oh,

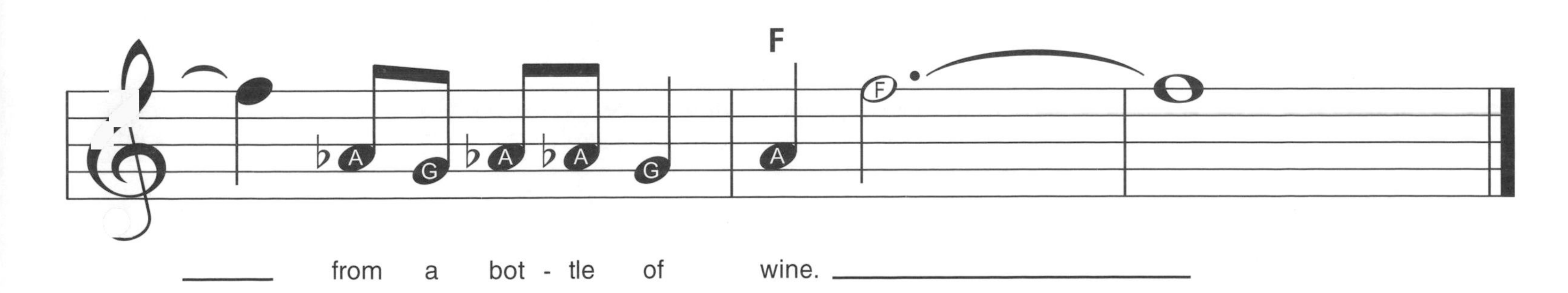
F
from a bot - tle of wine.

I Don't Wanna Go On with You Like That

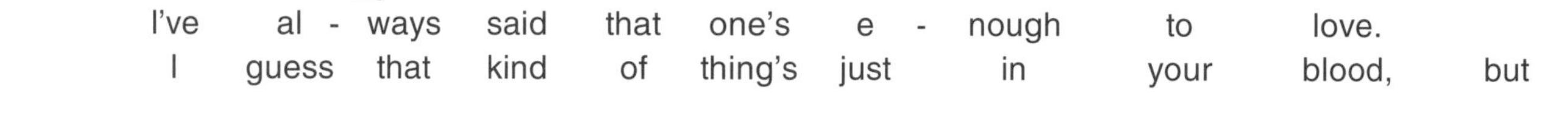

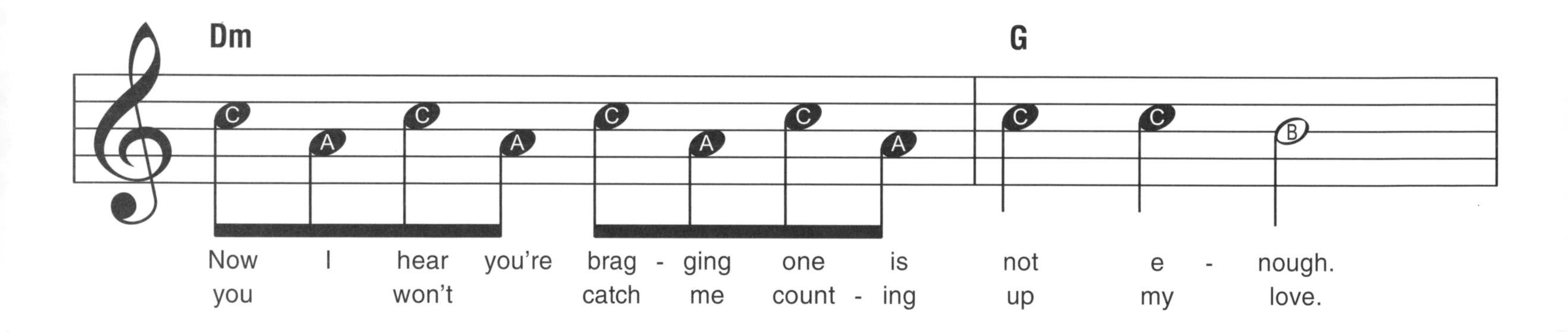

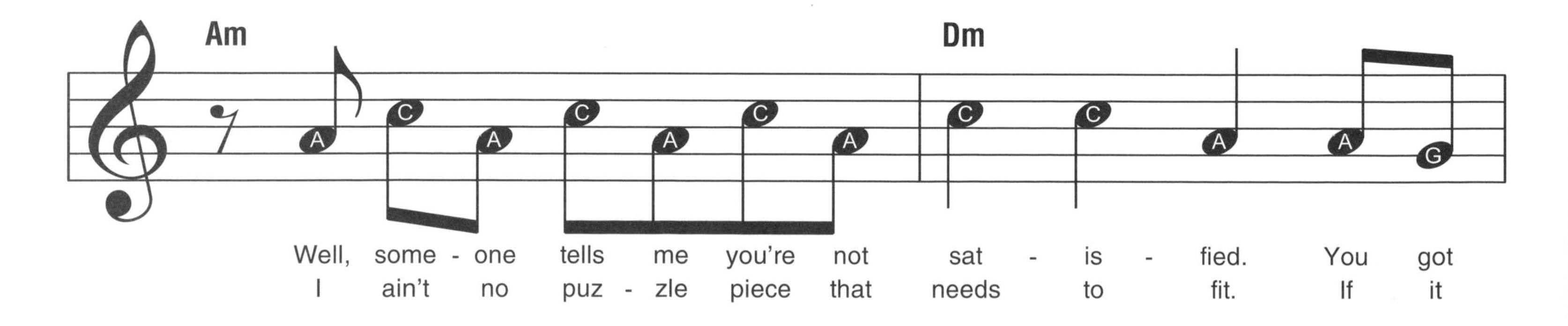

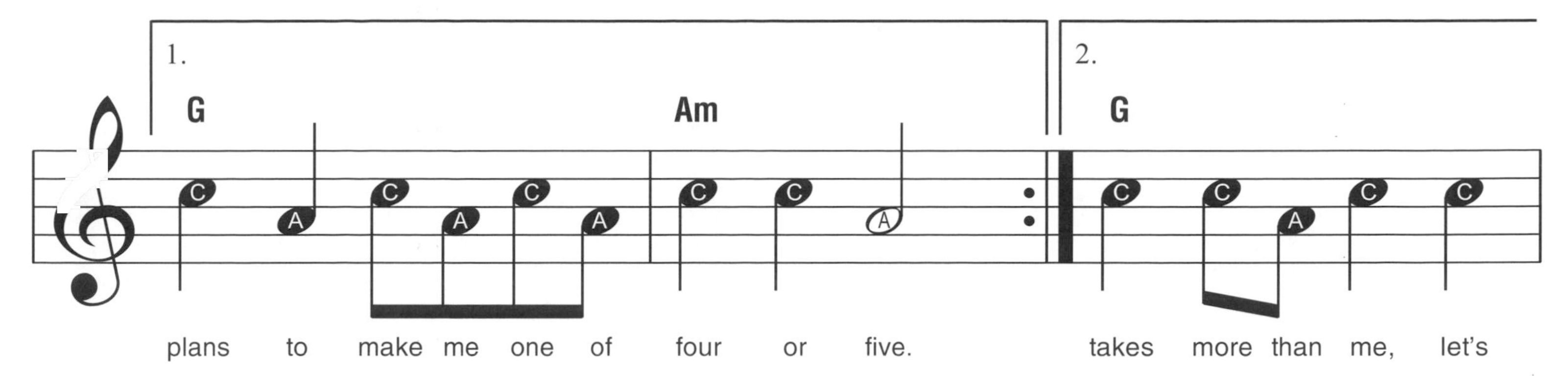
1.
2.
G
Am
G
plans to make me one of four or five.
takes more than me, let's

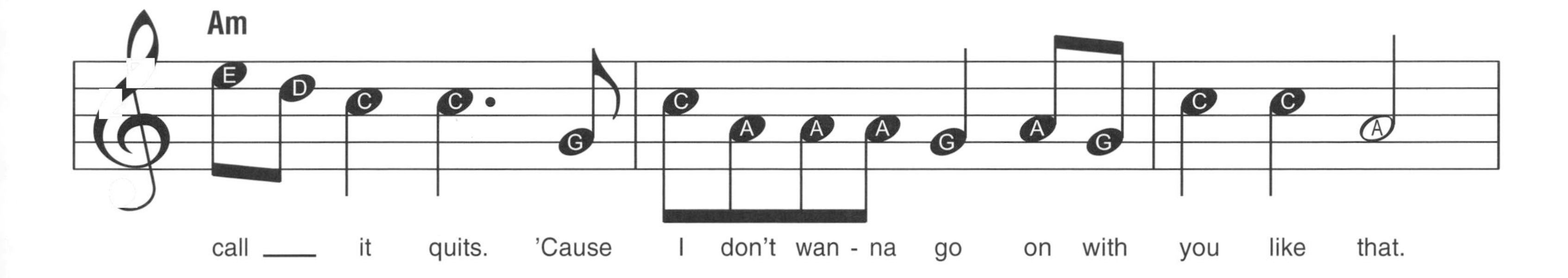
Am
call ___ it quits. 'Cause I don't wan - na go on with you like that.

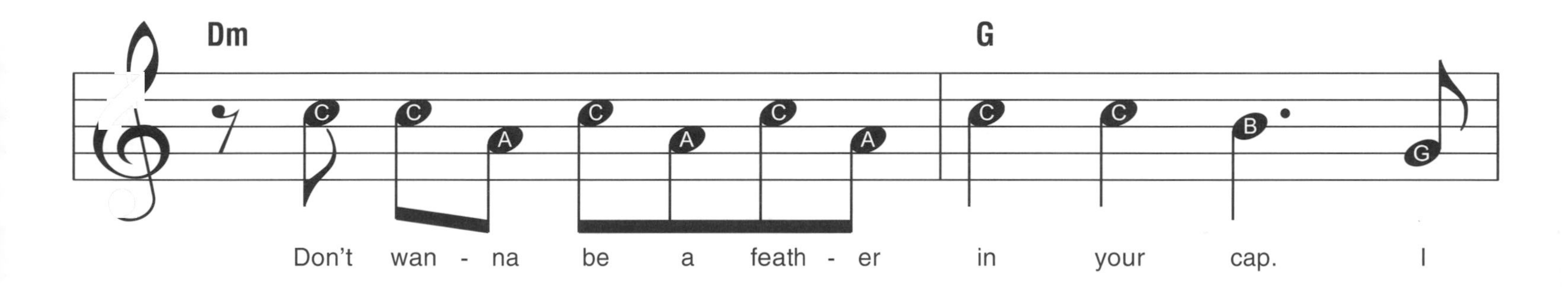
Dm
G
Don't wan - na be a feath - er in your cap. I

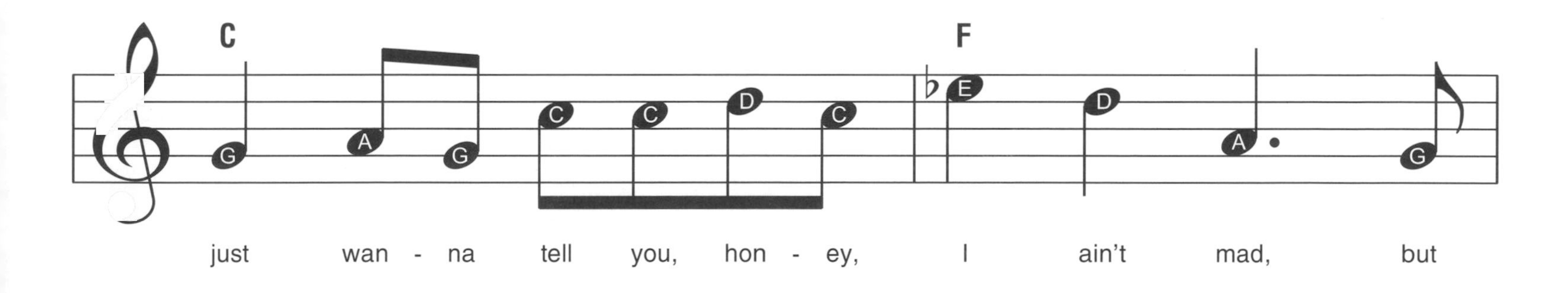
C
F
just wan - na tell you, hon - ey, I ain't mad, but

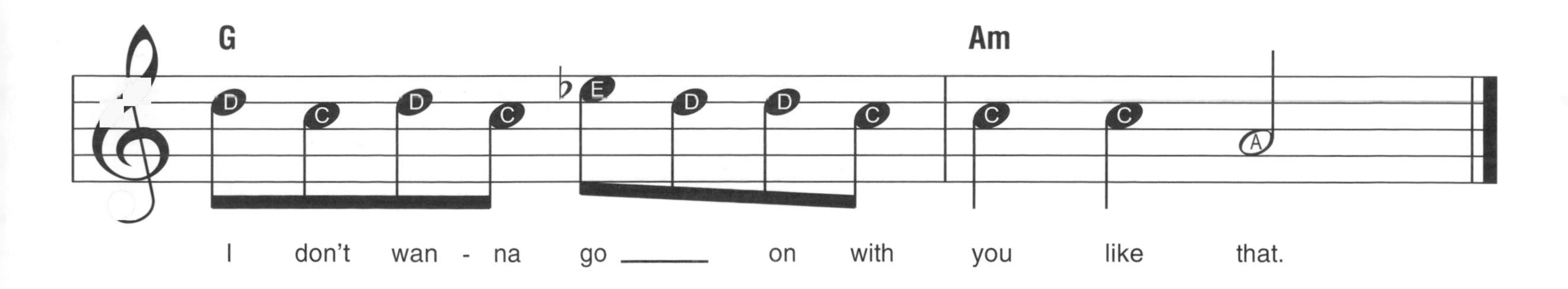
G
Am
I don't wan - na go ____ on with you like that.

I Guess That's Why
They Call It the Blues
G Em F C
Bm B7 G7 Am D
Words and Music by Elton John,
Bernie Taupin and Davey Johnstone
Moderately slow
Don't wish it a - way, don't look at it like it's for - ev - er.
Be - tween you and me, I could hon - est - ly say that things can on - ly get bet - ter.
And while I'm a - way, dust out the de - mons in -

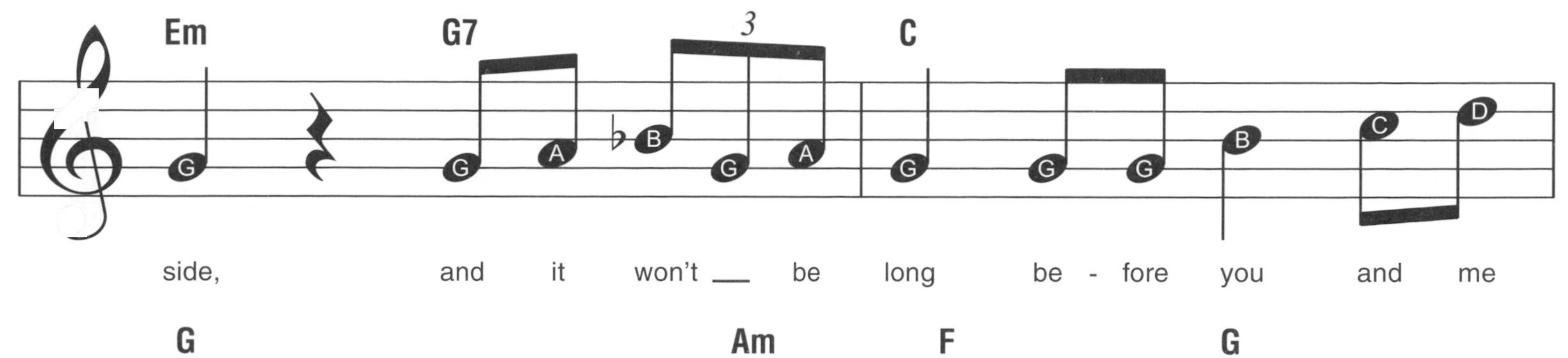
Em G7 C
3
side, and it won't __ be long be - fore you and me

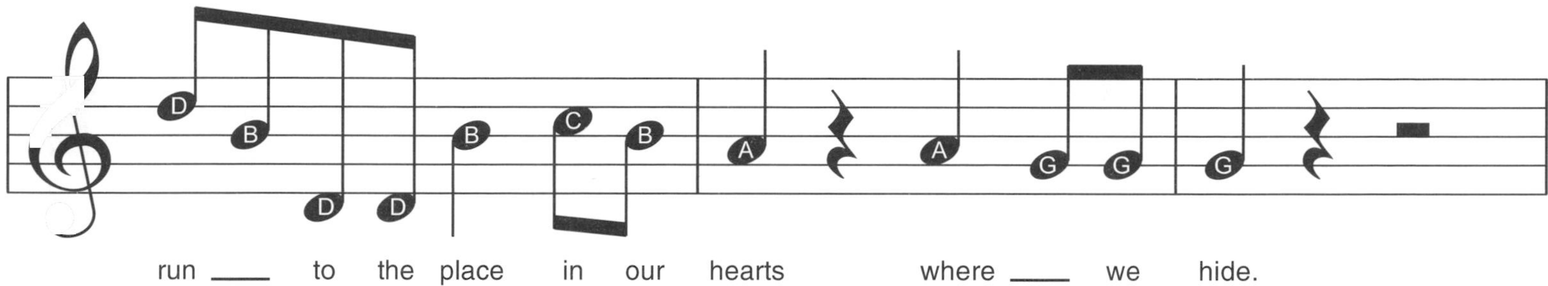
G Am F G
run __ to the place in our hearts where __ we hide.

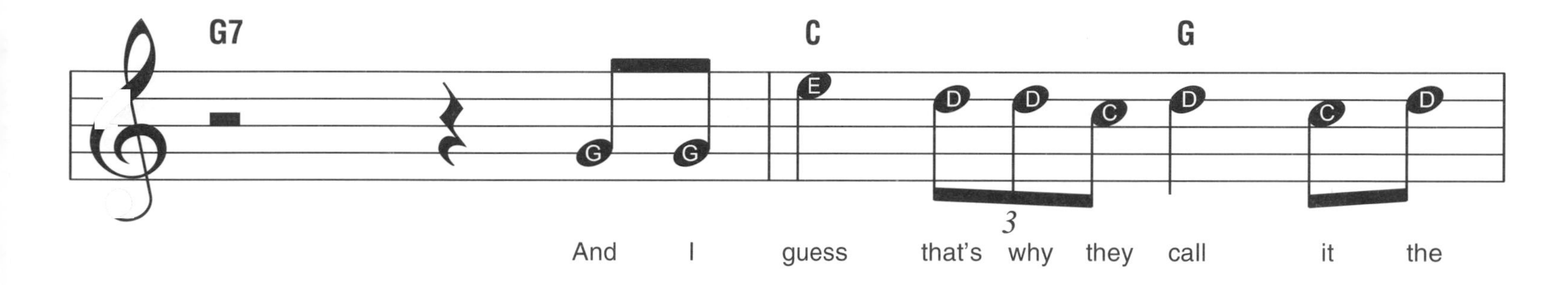
G7 C G
3
And I guess that's why they call it the

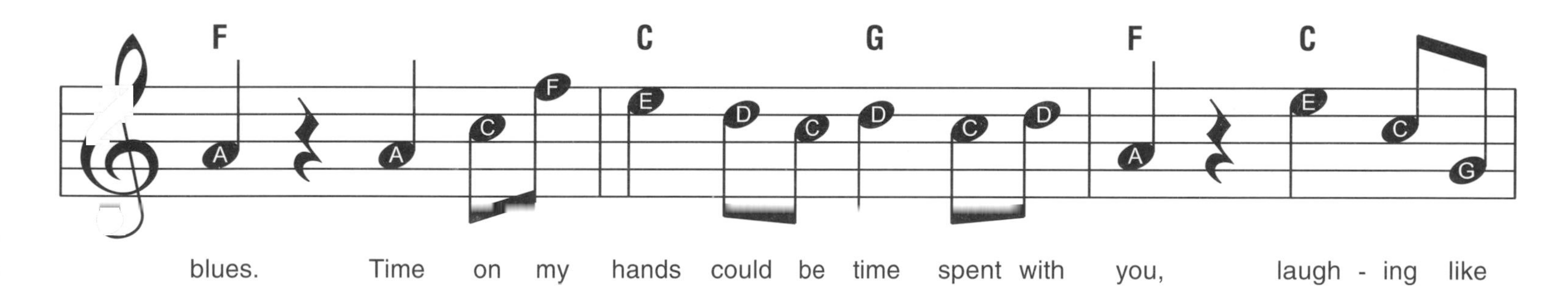
F C G F C
blues. Time on my hands could be time spent with you, laugh - ing like

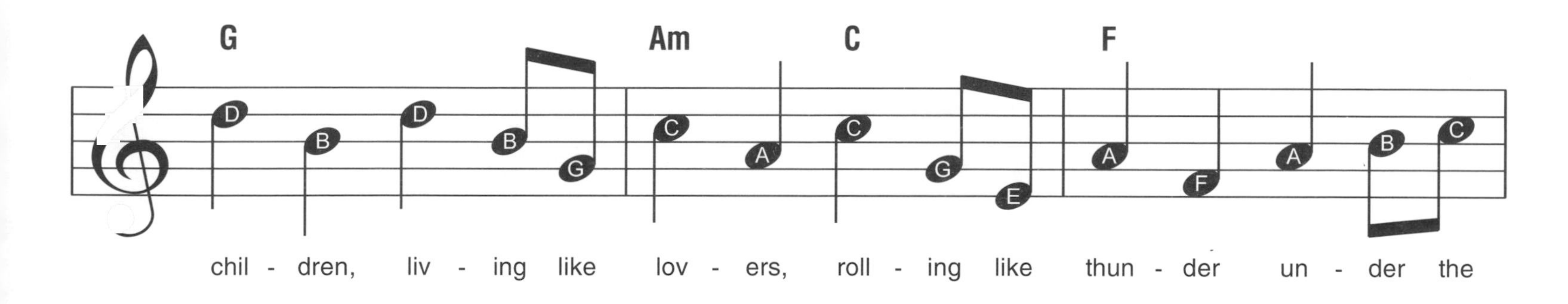
G Am C F
chil - dren, liv - ing like lov - ers, roll - ing like thun - der un - der the

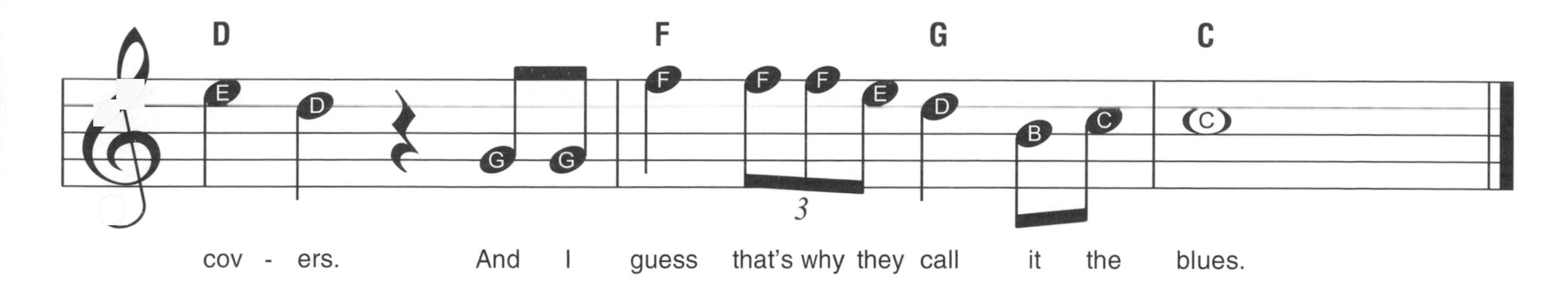
D F G C
3
cov - ers. And I guess that's why they call it the blues.

I'm Still Standing

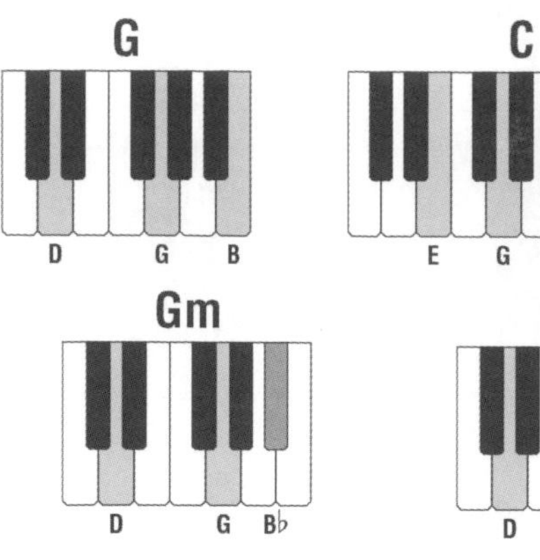
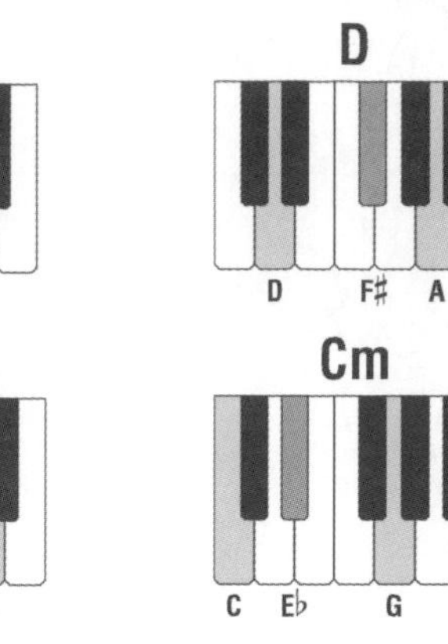
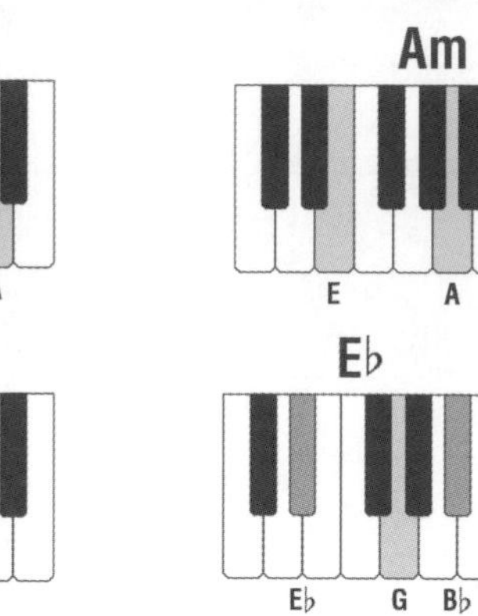
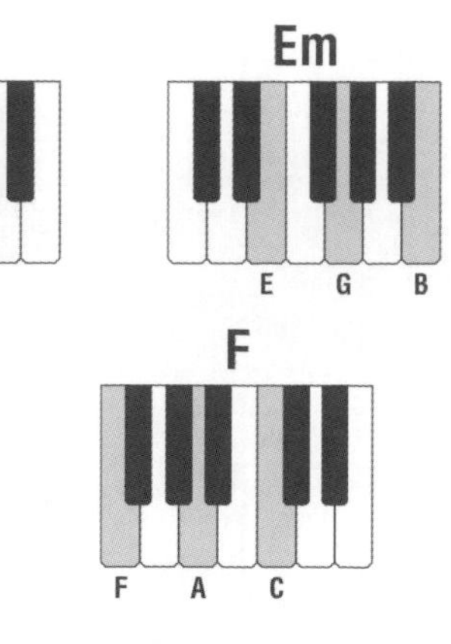

Words and Music by Elton John
and Bernie Taupin

Dm
stand - in' bet - ter than I ev - er did,
look - in' like a
stand - in' af - ter all this time,
pick - in' up the
Cm
1.
E♭
true sur - vi - vor,
feel - in' like a lit - tle kid.
piec - es of my
F
2.
D
And
life with - out you on my mind.
Gm
Cm
I'm still stand - in',
yeah, yeah,
D
Gm
yeah.
I'm still stand - in',
Cm
D
Gm
yeah, yeah, yeah.
I'm still stand - in'.

Nikita

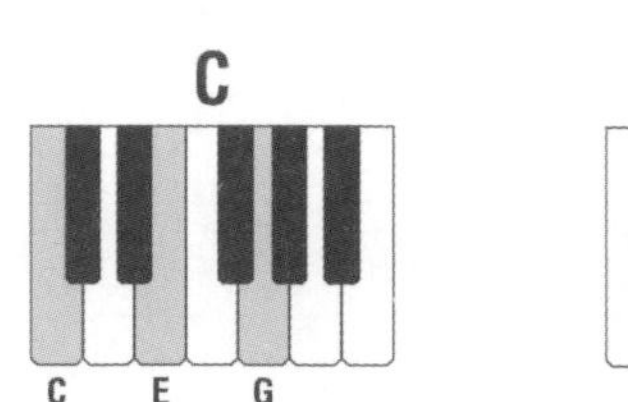

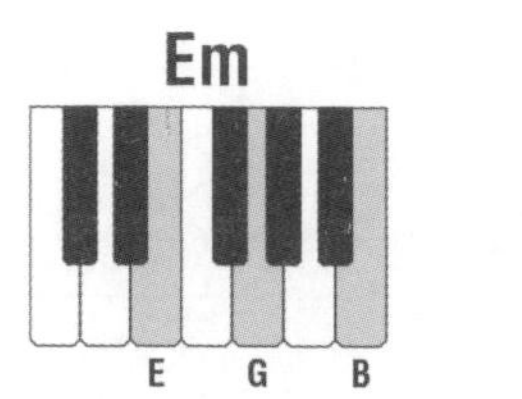

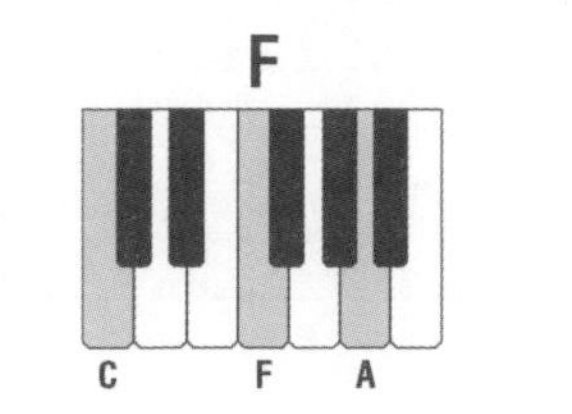

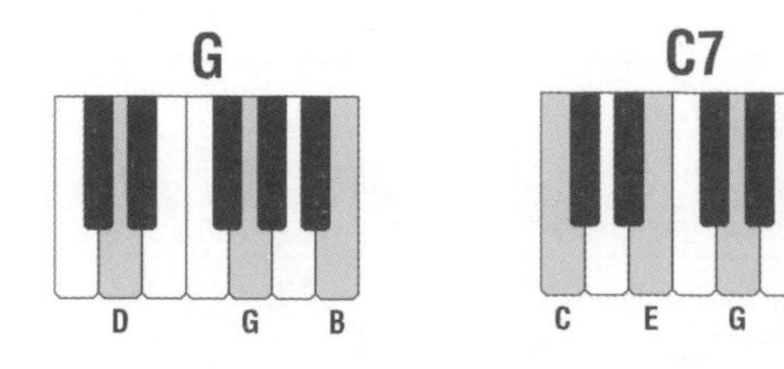

Words and Music by Elton John
and Bernie Taupin

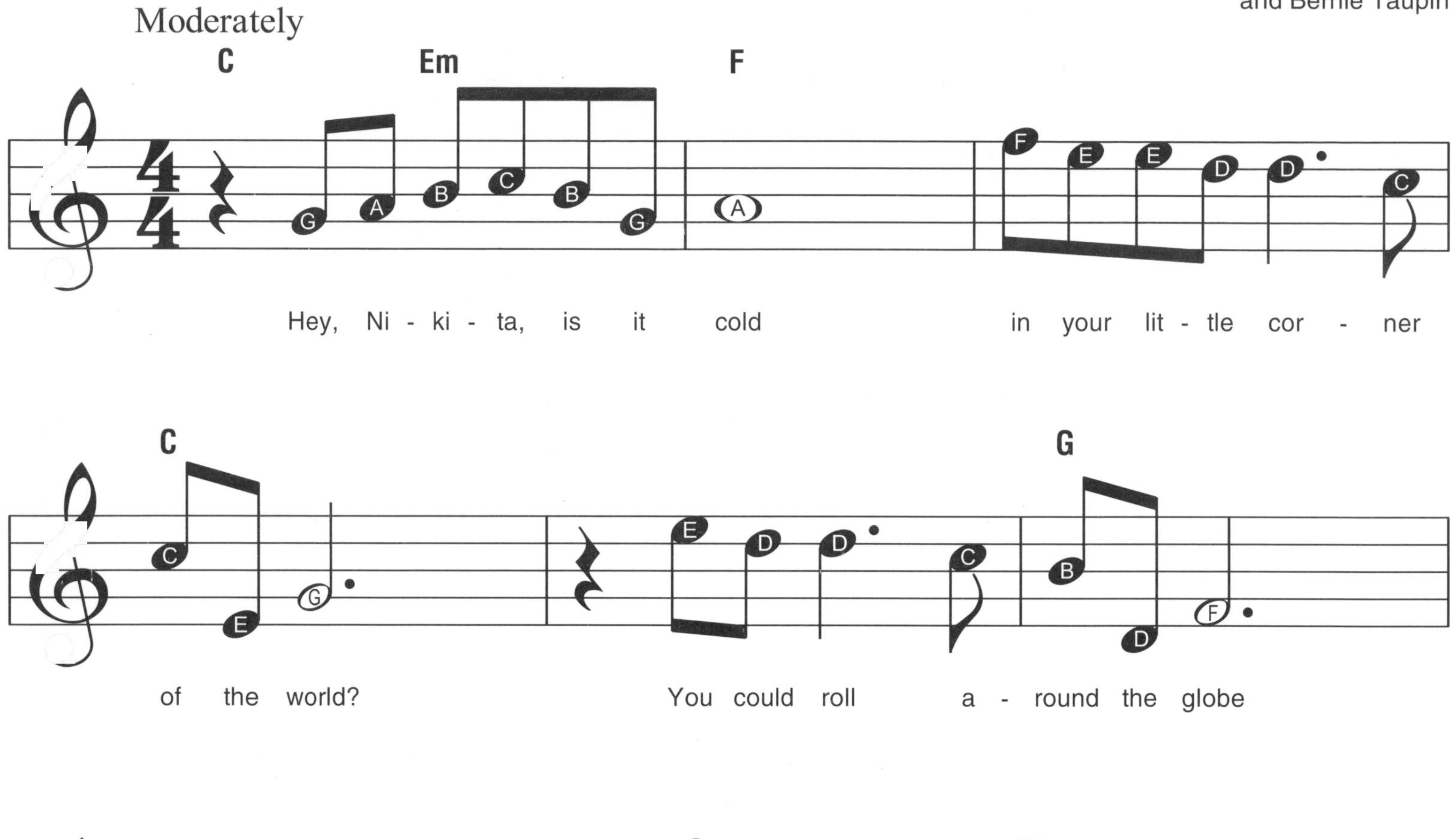

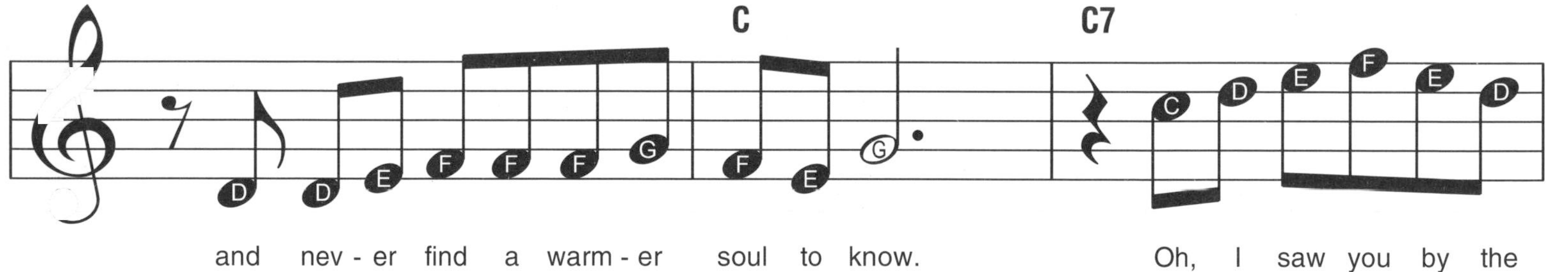

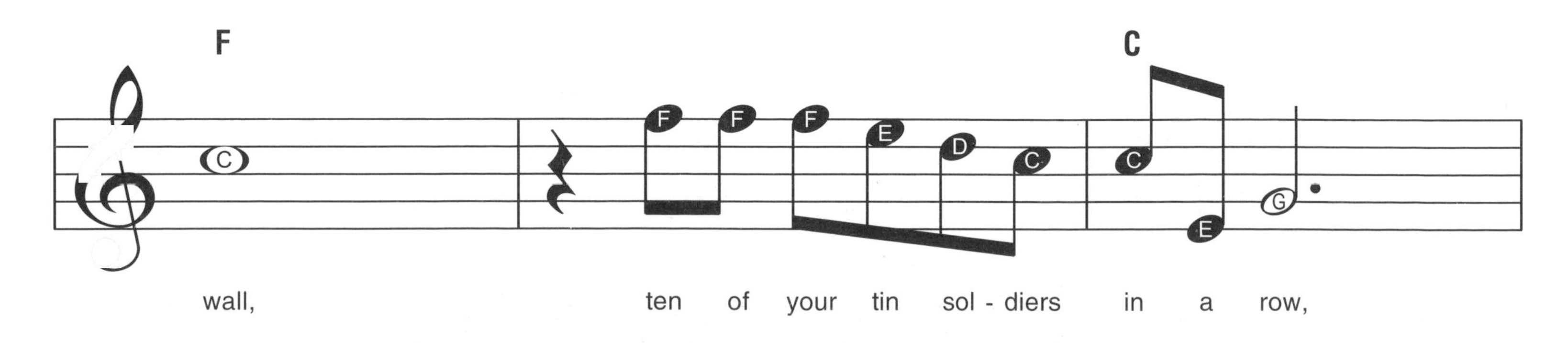

G
with eyes that looked like ice on fire,
the hu - man heart a cap - tive
C
C7
in the snow.
Oh, Ni - ki - ta, you will
Oh, Ni - ki - ta, is the
F
C
nev - er know
an - y - thing a - bout my home.
I'll
oth - er side
of an - y giv - en line in time
1.
G
nev - er know how good it feels to hold you.
count - ing ten tin sol - diers in a
C
2.
G
Ni - ki - ta, I need you so.
row?
Oh
C
no, Ni - ki - ta, you'll nev - er know.

Philadelphia Freedom

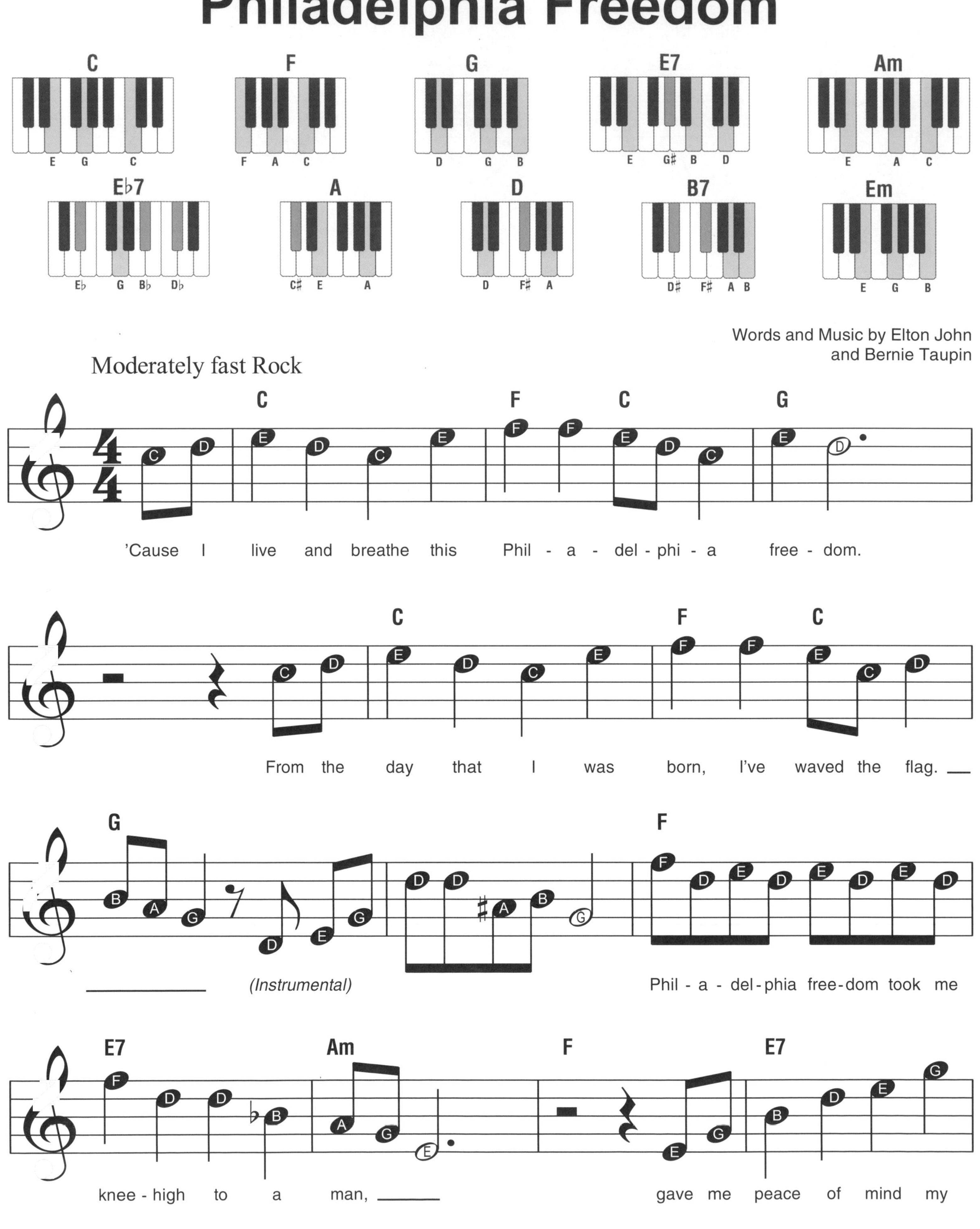

Words and Music by Elton John
and Bernie Taupin

E♭7 C G
dad - dy nev - er had. Oh, Phil - a - del - phi - a
C G Am
free - dom, shine on me. I love you. Shine the light through the
G A D B7 Em
eyes of the ones left be - hind. Shine the light, shine
Am G F
the light. Shine the light, won't you shine the light.
C Am C D C G
Phil - a - del - phi - a free - dom, I love
Am G
you, yes, I do. (Instrumental)

Rocket Man
(I Think It's Gonna Be a Long Long Time)
Em
E G B
A7
E G A C♯
G
D G B
C
E G C
Am
E A C
D
D F♯ A
Words and Music by Elton John
and Bernie Taupin
Moderate Ballad
Em
A7
She packed my bags last night pre - flight.
I miss the earth so much. I miss my wife.
Em
Ze - ro hour, nine A. M.
It's lone - ly out in space
A7
G
C
And I'm gon - na be
on such a
G
Am
high as a kite by
time - less flight.

D
G
then.
And I think it's gon - na
C
be a long, long time till touch - down brings me 'round a - gain to
G
C
find I'm not the man they think I am at home. Oh, no, no,
G
A7
C
no. I'm a rock - et man,
rock - et man,

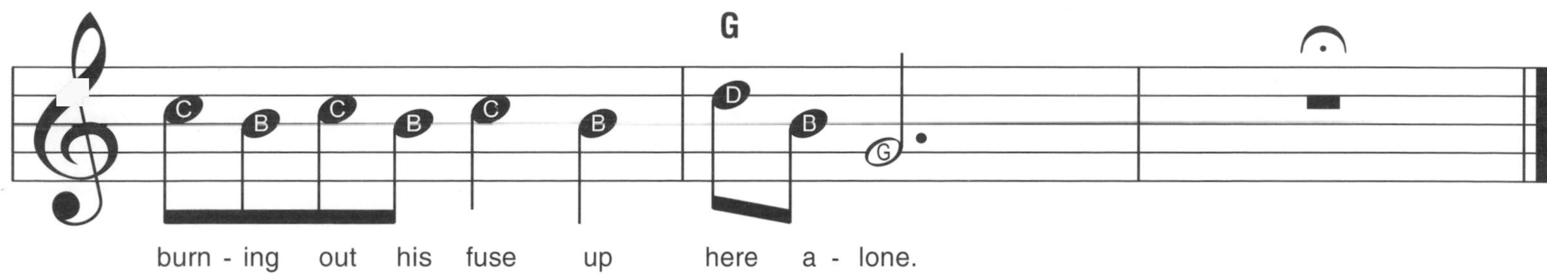
G
burn - ing out his fuse up here a - lone.

Sacrifice

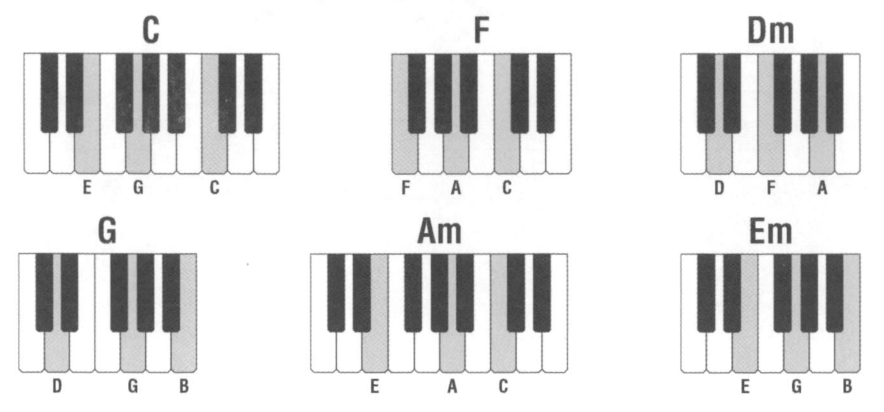

Words and Music by Elton John
and Bernie Taupin

Moderately fast

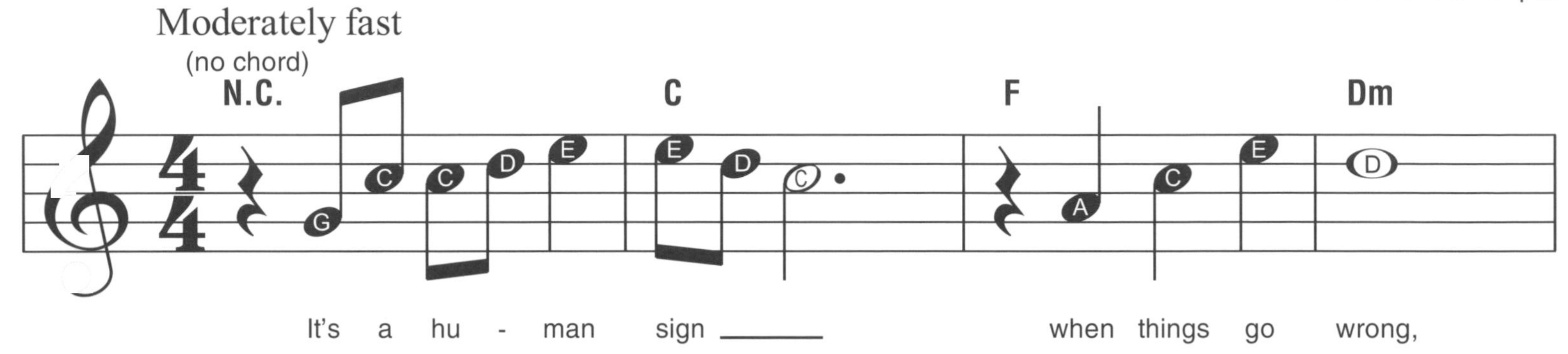

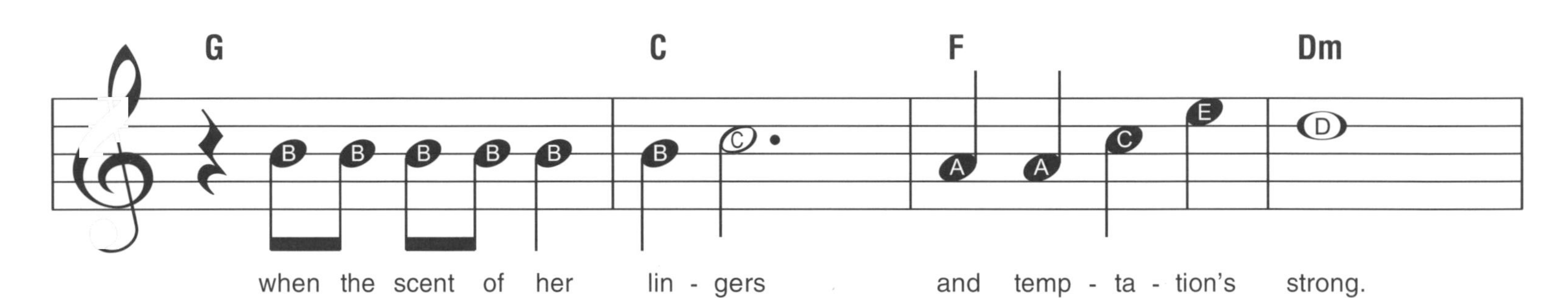

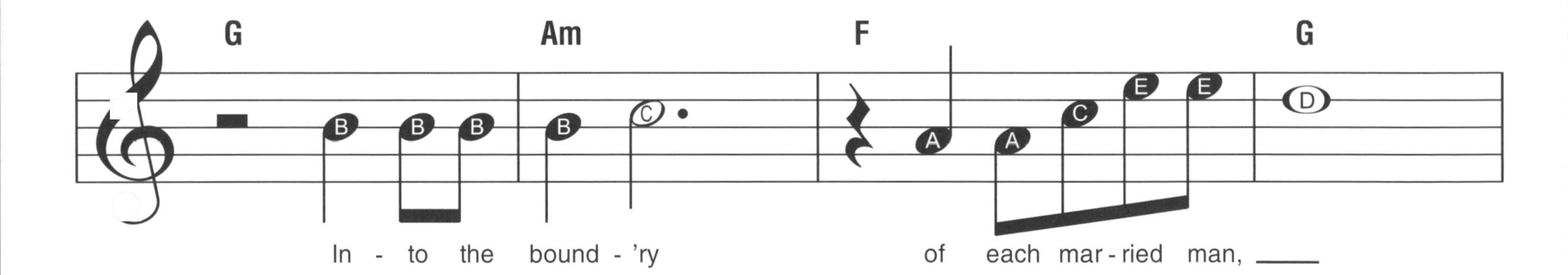

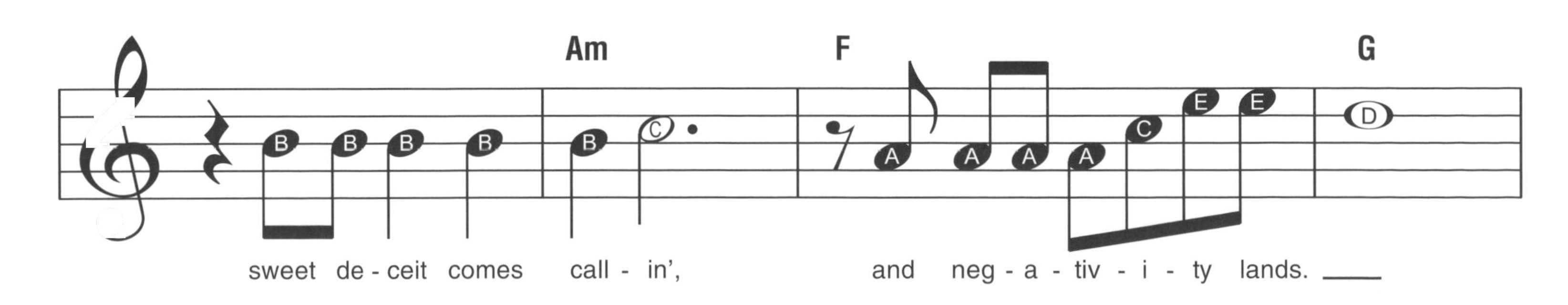

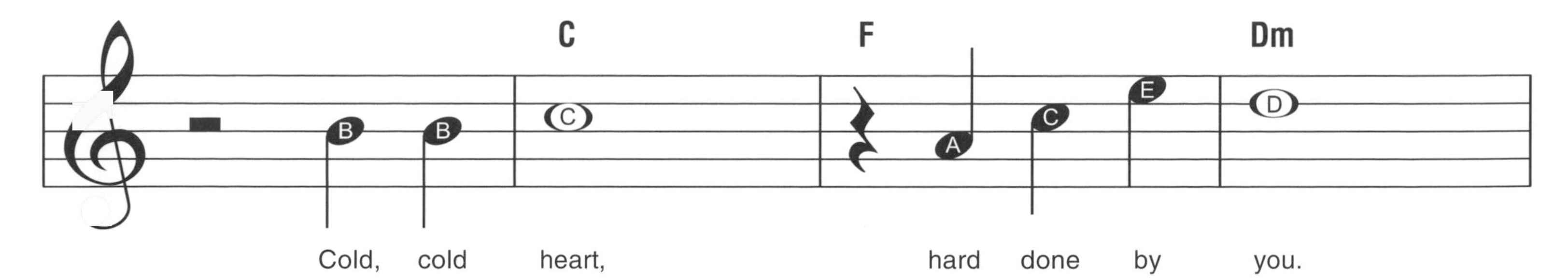
C F Dm
Cold, cold heart, hard done by you.

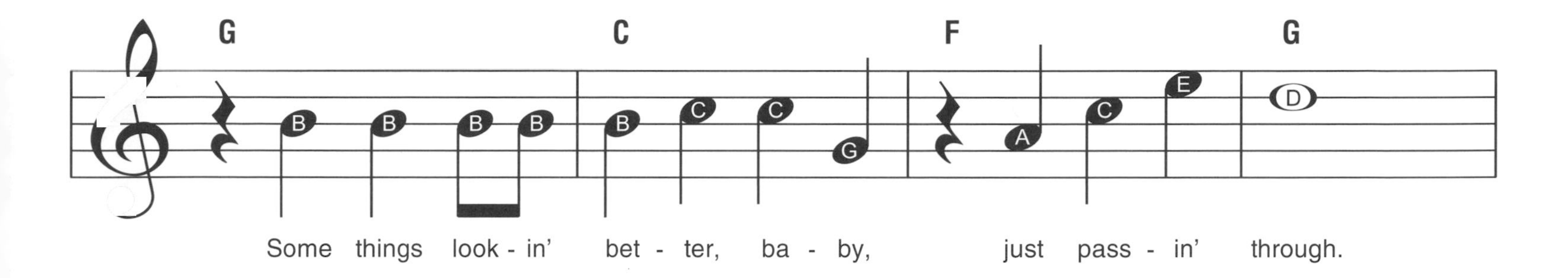
G C F G
Some things look - in' bet - ter, ba - by, just pass - in' through.

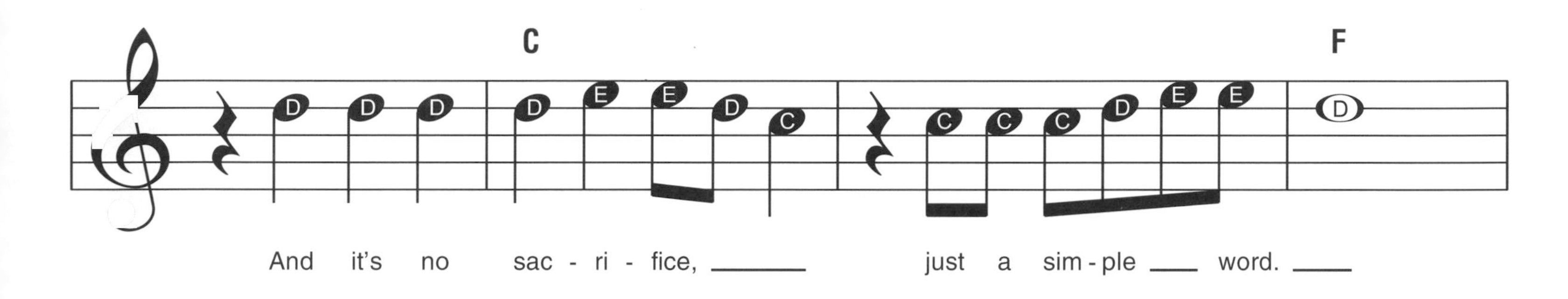
C F
And it's no sac - ri - fice, just a sim - ple word.

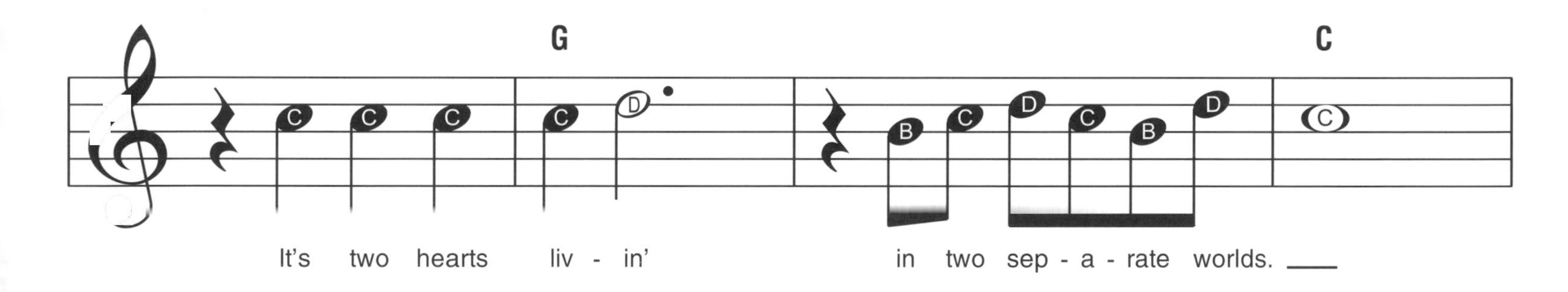
G C
It's two hearts liv - in' in two sep - a - rate worlds.

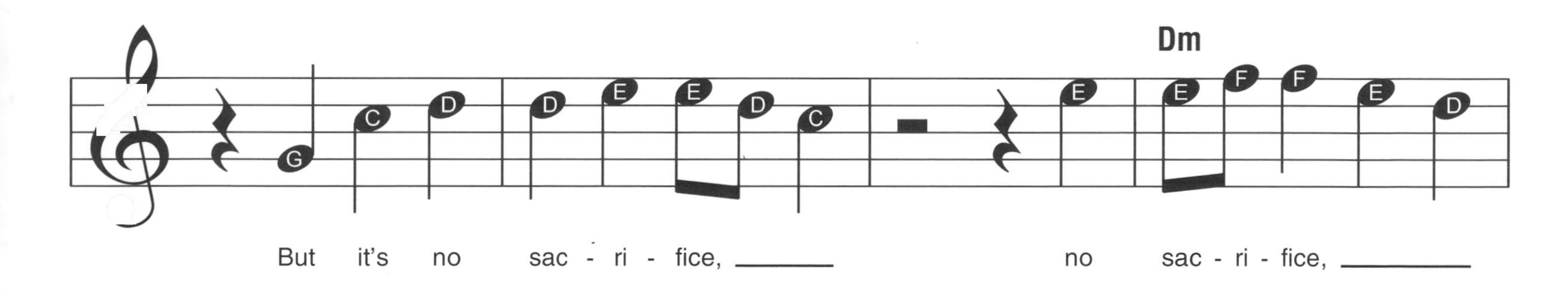
Dm
But it's no sac - ri - fice, no sac - ri - fice,

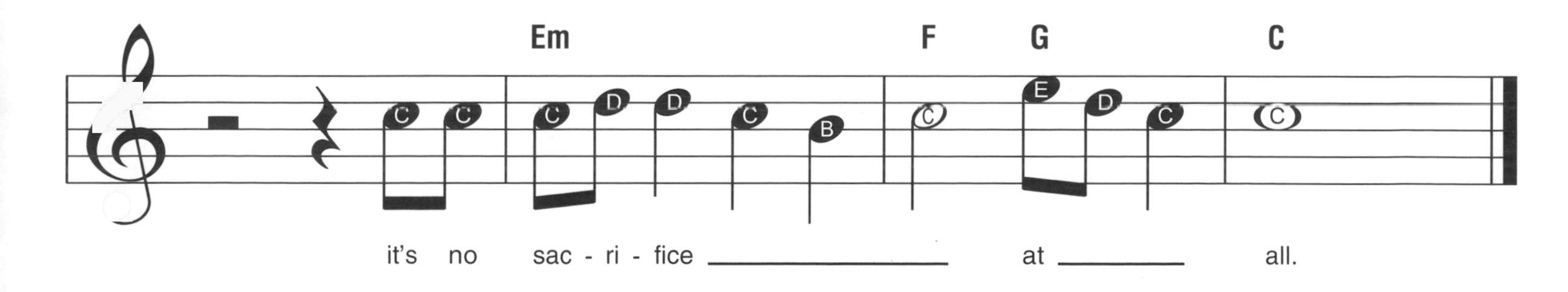
Em F G C
it's no sac - ri - fice at all.

Sad Songs
(Say So Much)

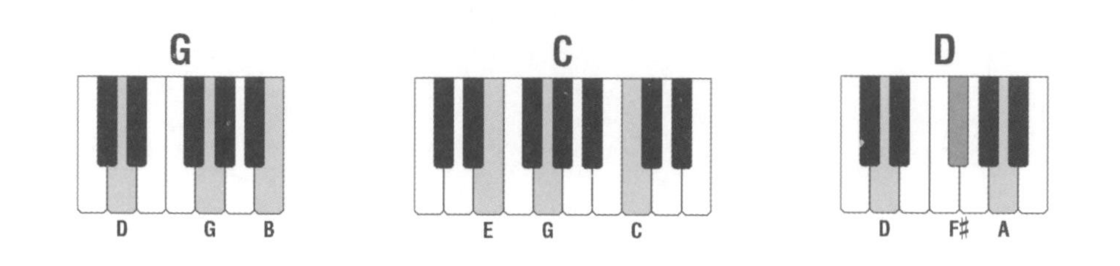

Words and Music by Elton John
and Bernie Taupin

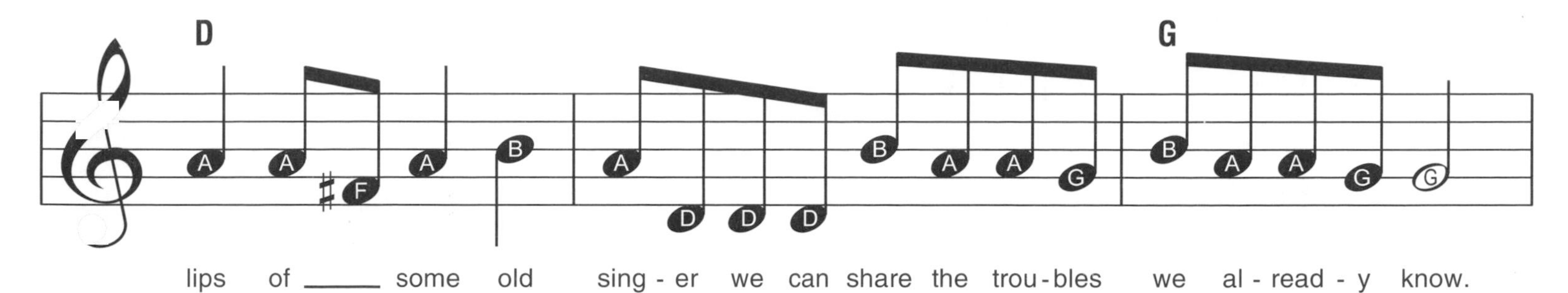
D
G
lips of ___ some old sing - er we can share the trou - bles we al - read - y know.

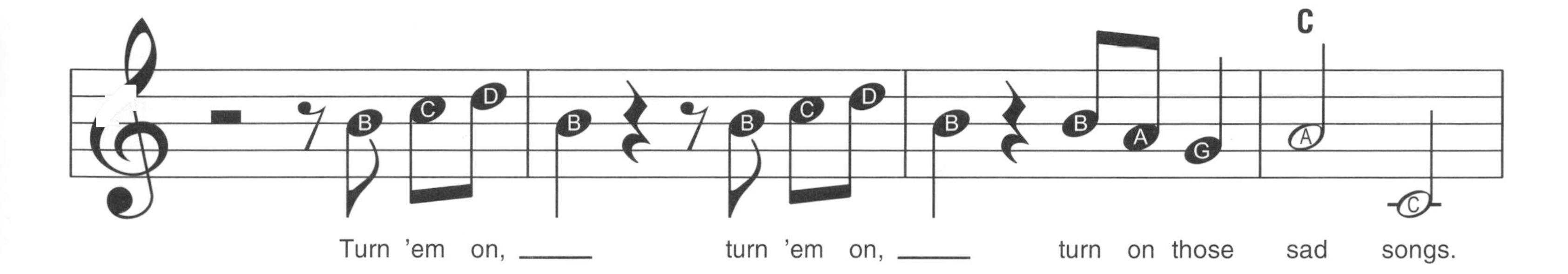
C
Turn 'em on, ___ turn 'em on, ___ turn on those sad songs.

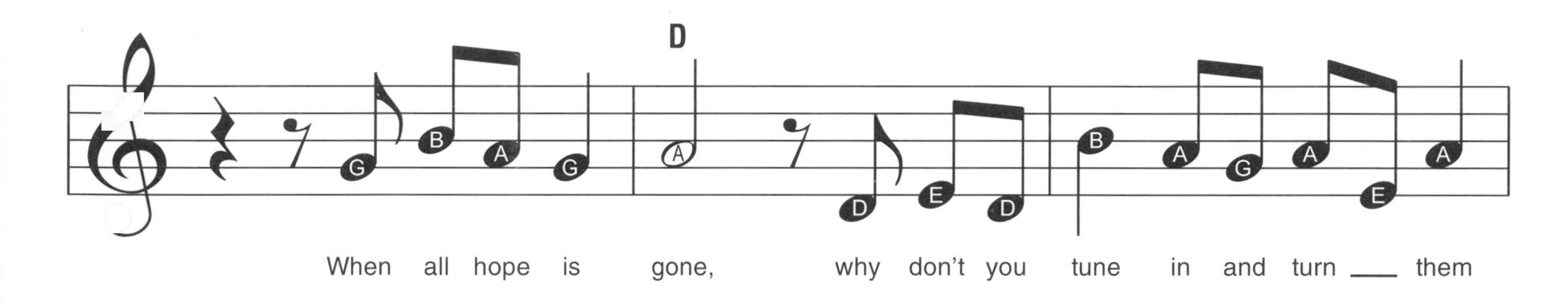
D
When all hope is gone, why don't you tune in and turn ___ them

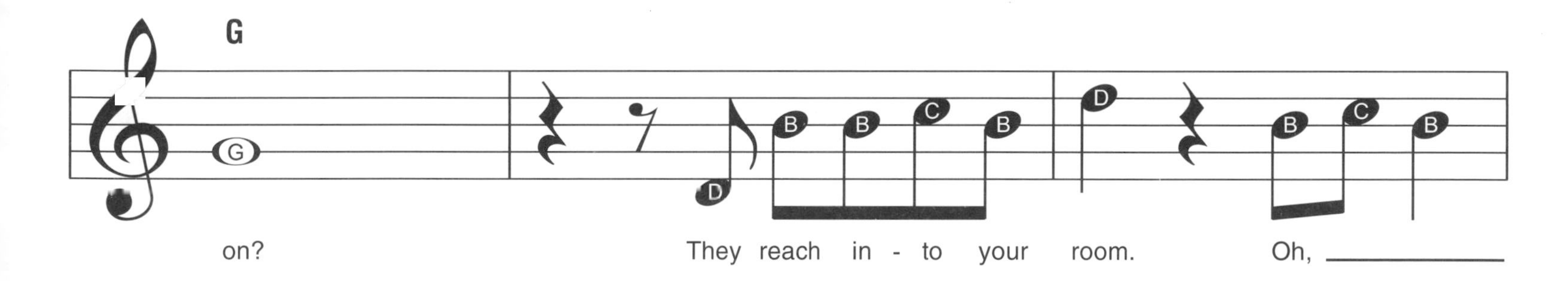
G
on? They reach in - to your room. Oh, ___

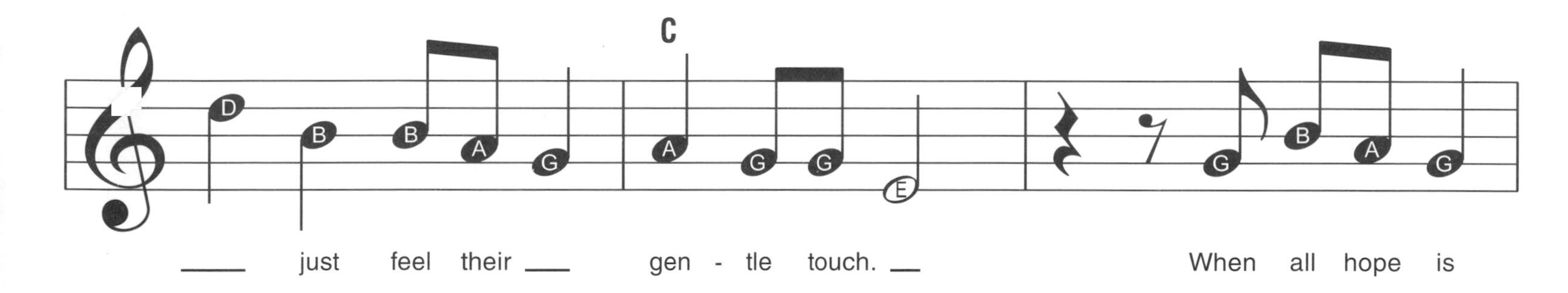
C
___ just feel their ___ gen - tle touch. ___ When all hope is

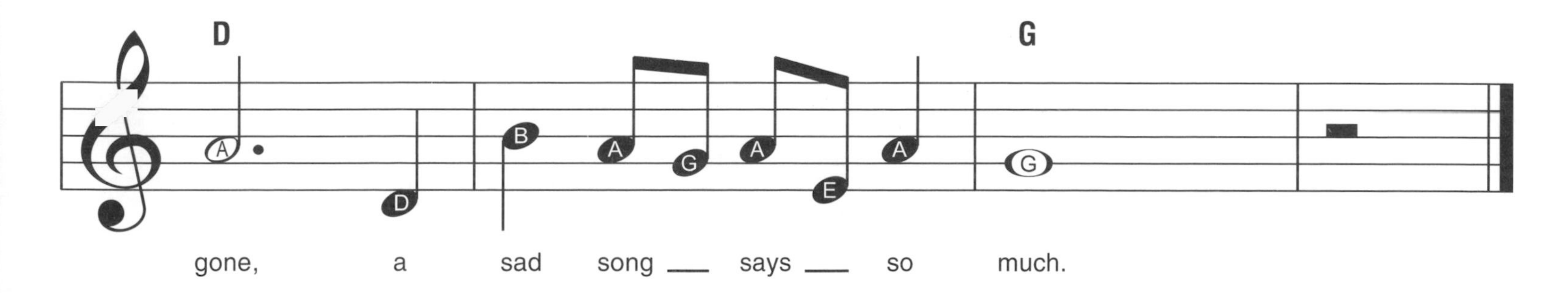
D
G
gone, a sad song ___ says ___ so much.

Something About the Way You Look Tonight

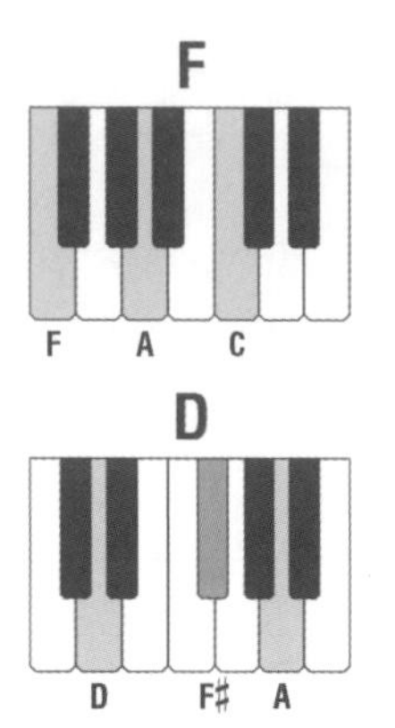

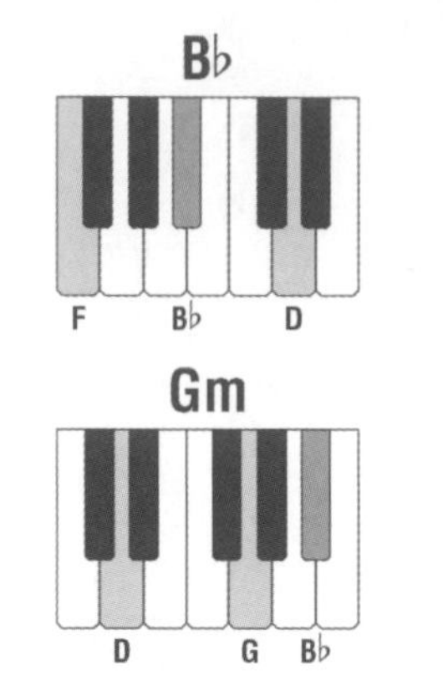

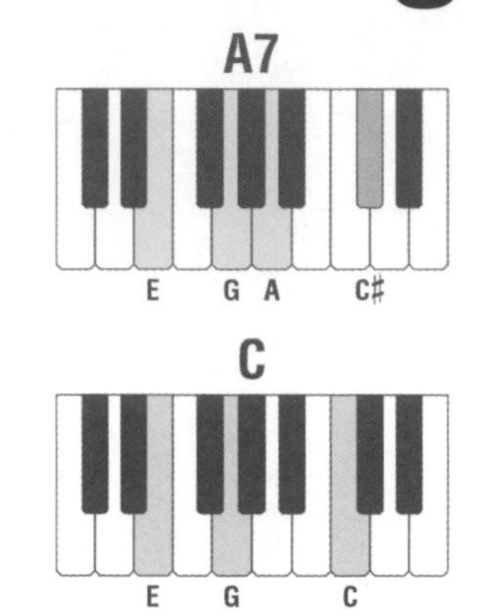

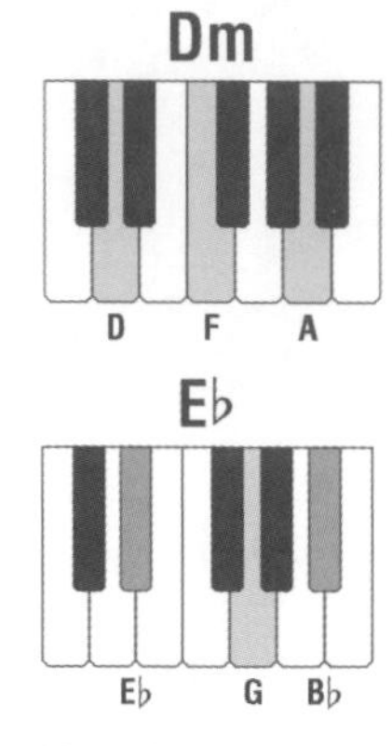

Words and Music by Elton John
and Bernie Taupin

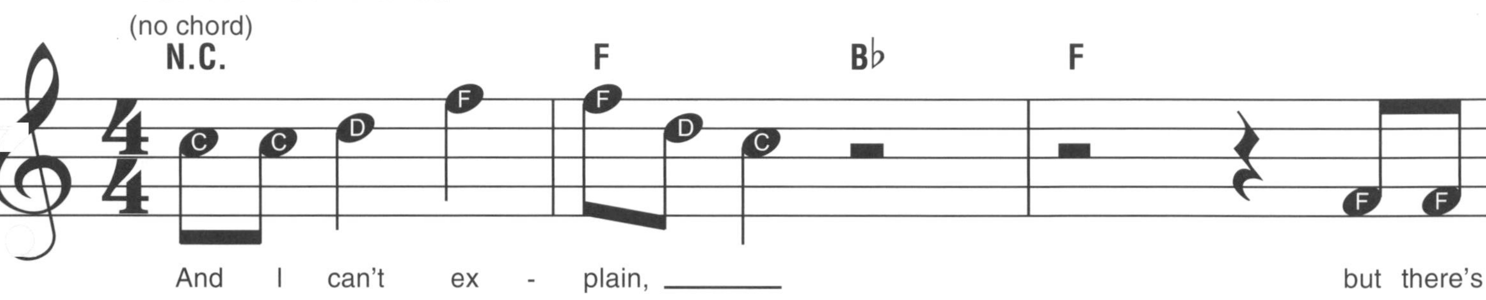

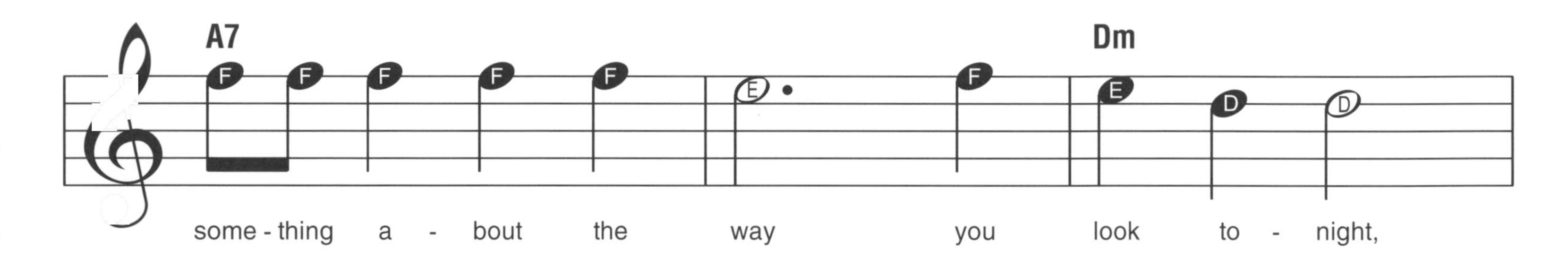

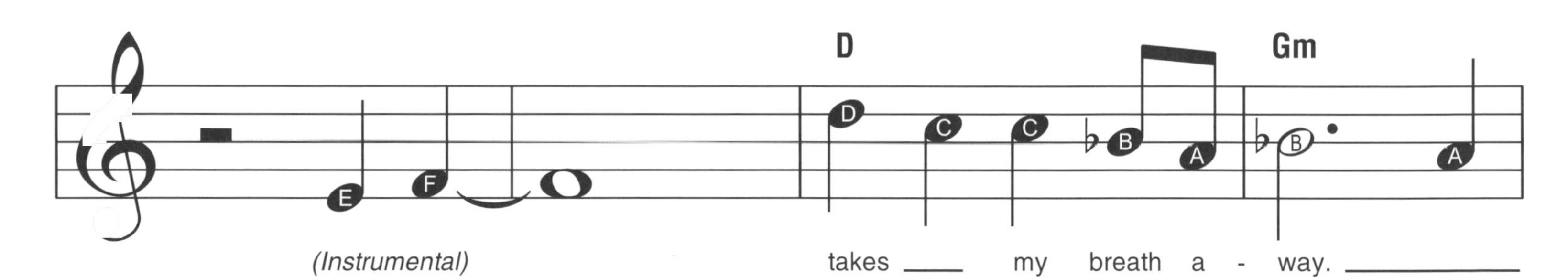

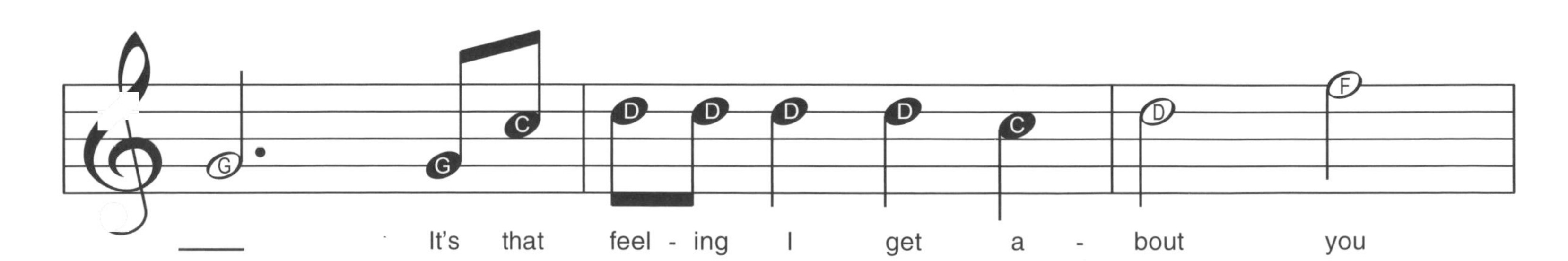

C F C
deep in - side.
(Instrumental)
F B♭ F
And I can't de - scribe,
but there's
A7 Dm
some - thing a - bout the way you look to - night,
B♭ C
(Instrumental)
takes my breath a - way.
(Instrumental)
The way you look to -
F E♭ F
(Instrumental)

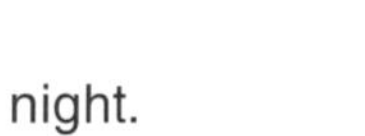
night.

Sorry Seems to Be the Hardest Word

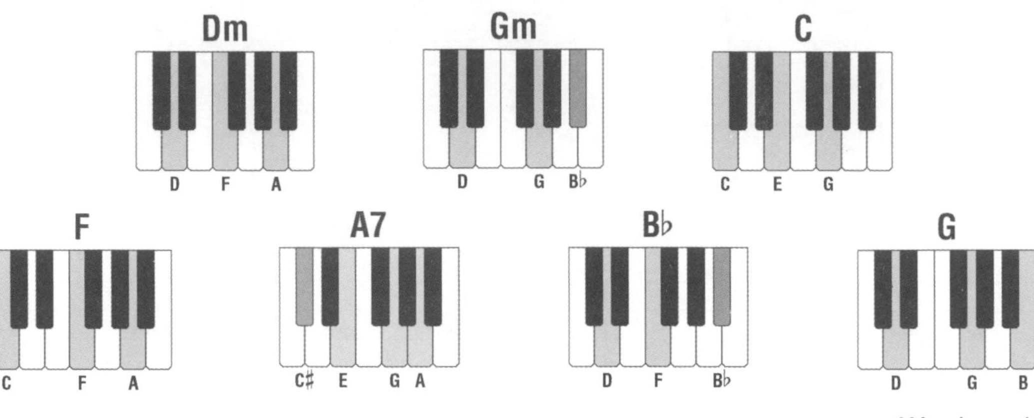

Words and Music by Elton John
and Bernie Taupin

F
Gm
A7
find that you're not there?
2.
C
and sor - ry seems to be the hard - est
F
C
B♭
A7
word?
It's sad, so sad.
It's sad, so sad.
F
G
1.
B♭
It's a sad, sad sit - u - a - tion,
Why can't we talk it o - ver?
and it's get - ting
A7
Dm
Gm
A7
2.
B♭
more and more ab - surd.
Oh, it seems to
Gm
A7
Dm
me that sor - ry seems to be the hard - est word.

Tiny Dancer

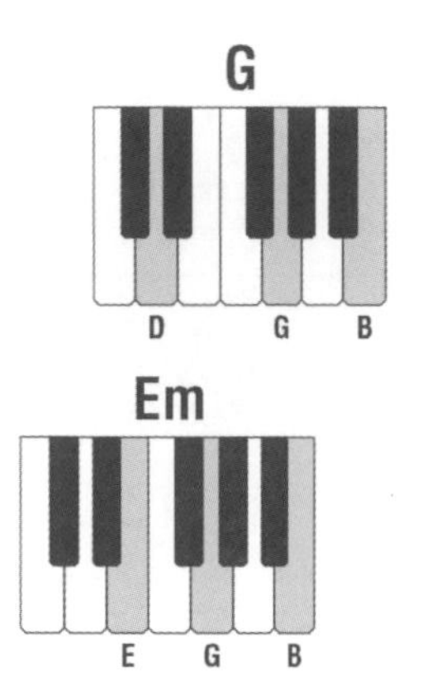

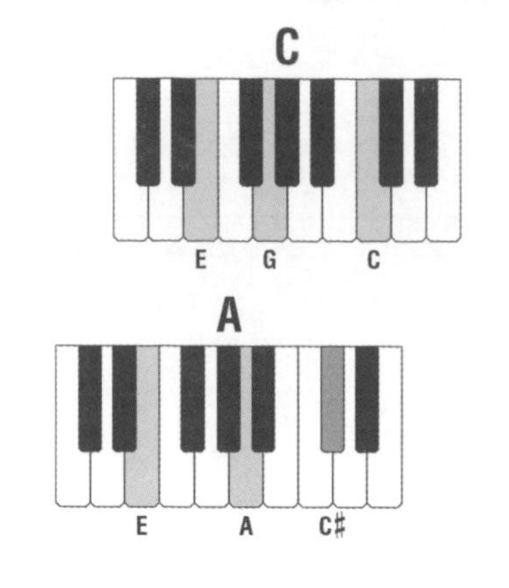

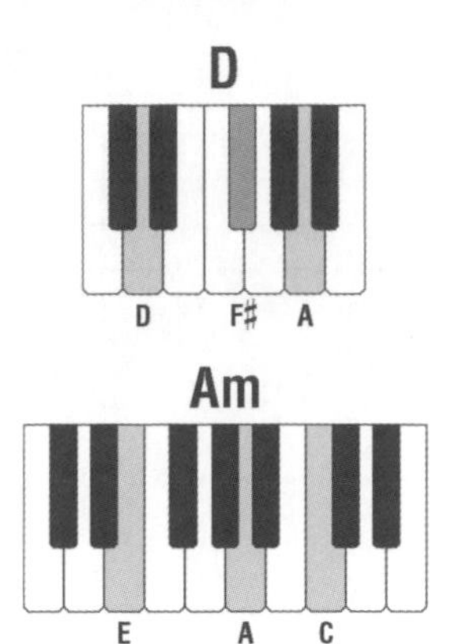

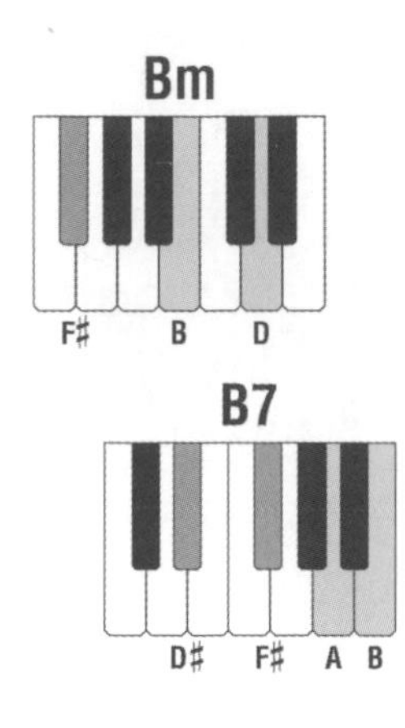

Words and Music by Elton John
and Bernie Taupin

Moderate Ballad

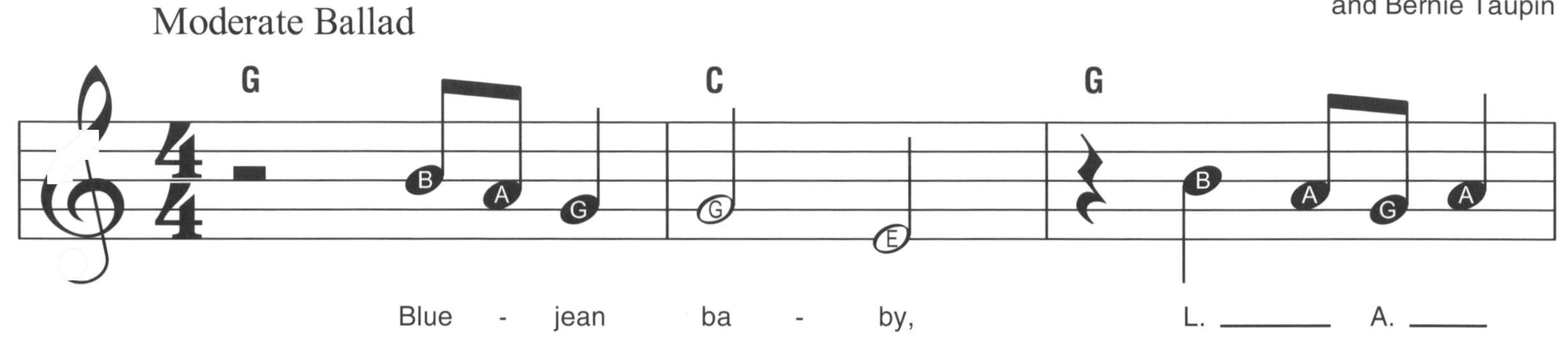

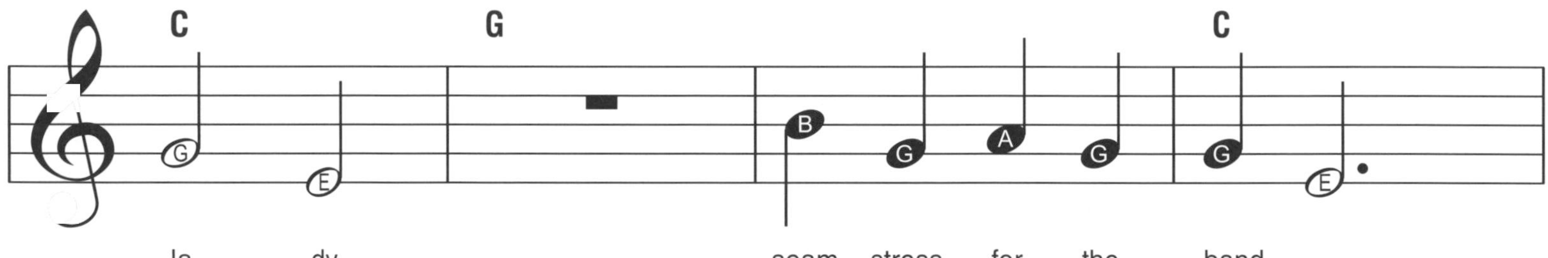

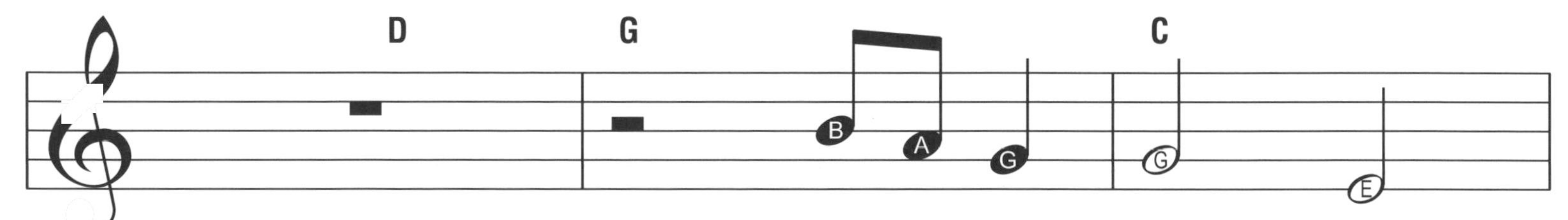

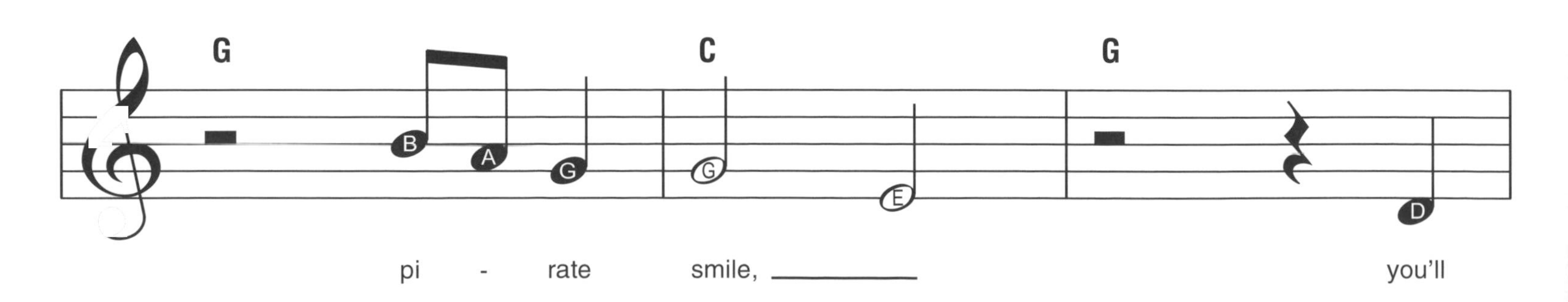

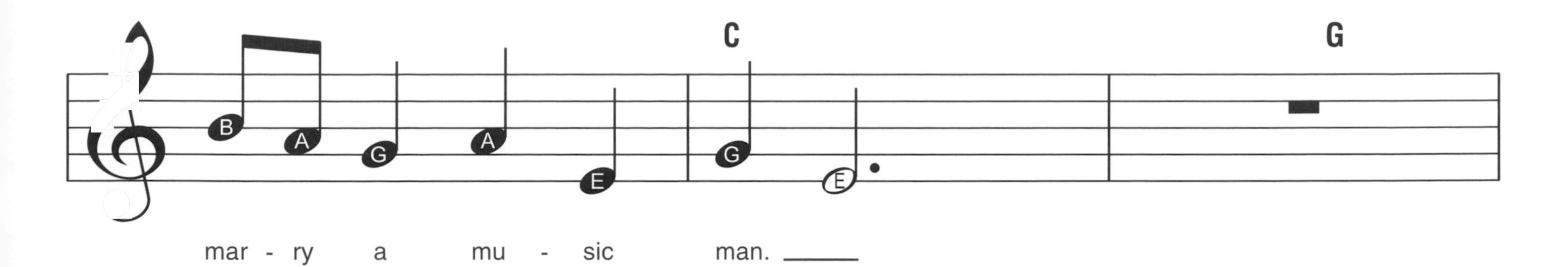
C
G
B
A
G
A
E
G
E
mar - ry a mu - sic man.

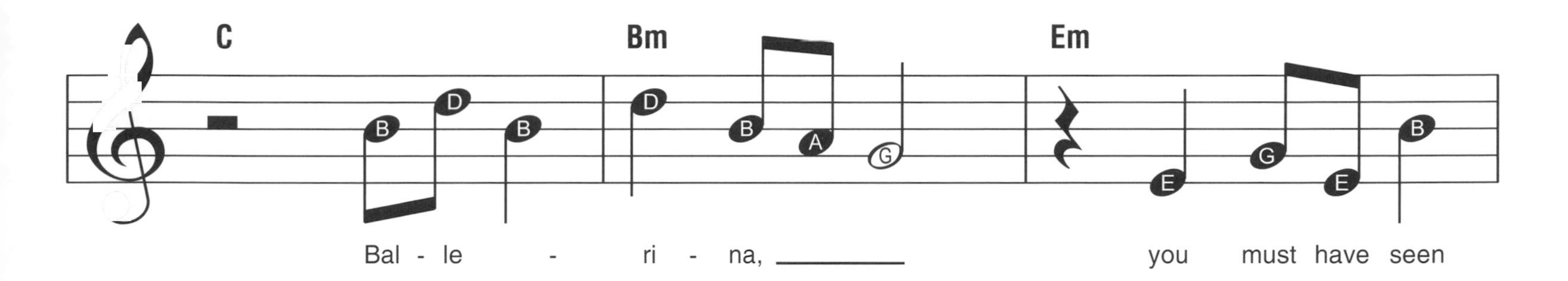
C
Bm
Em
B
D
B
D
B
A
G
E
G
E
B
Bal - le - ri - na,
you must have seen

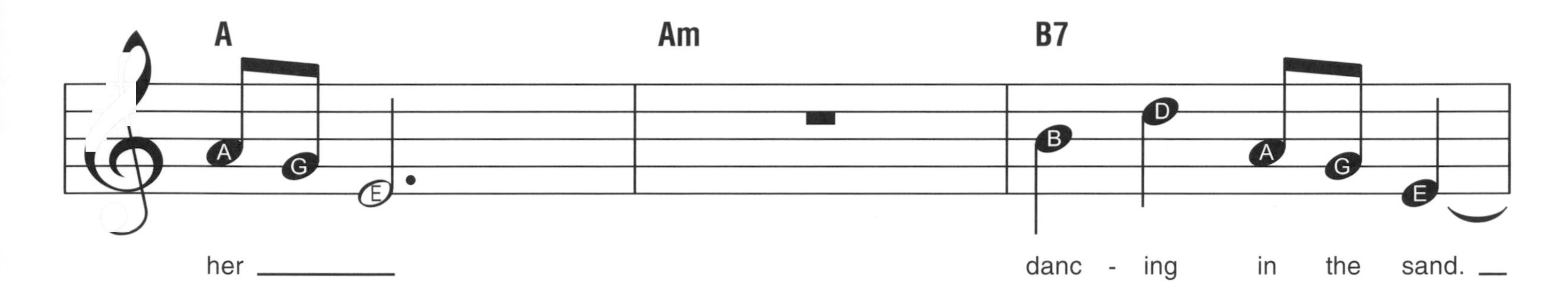
A
Am
B7
A
G
E
B
D
A
G
E
her
danc - ing in the sand.

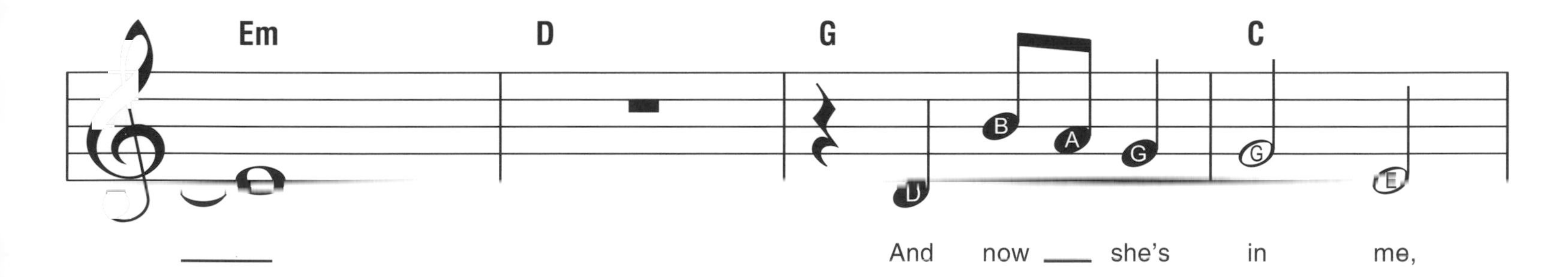
Em
D
G
C
D
B
A
G
G
E
And now she's in me,

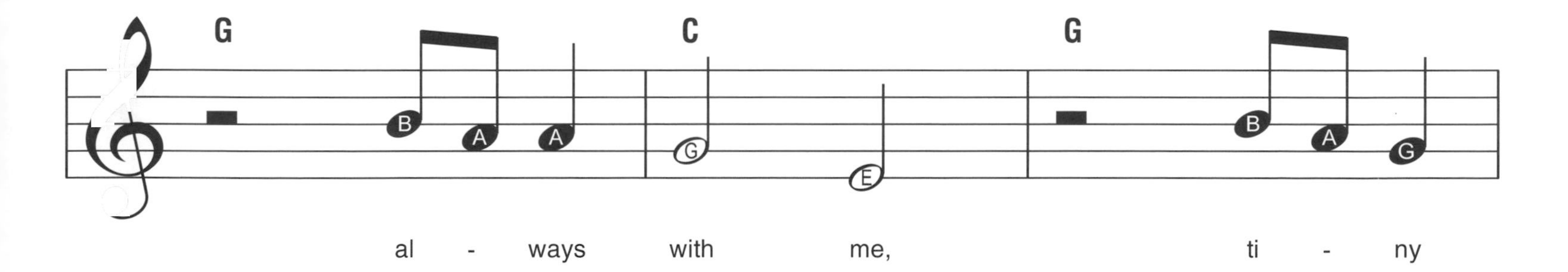
G
C
G
B
A
A
G
E
B
A
G
al - ways with me,
ti - ny

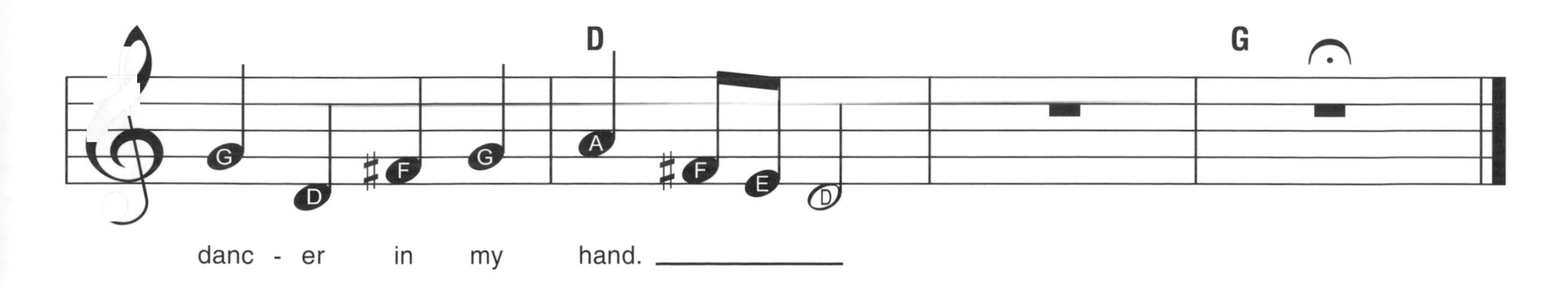
D
G
G
D
F
G
A
F
E
D
danc - er in my hand.

Your Song

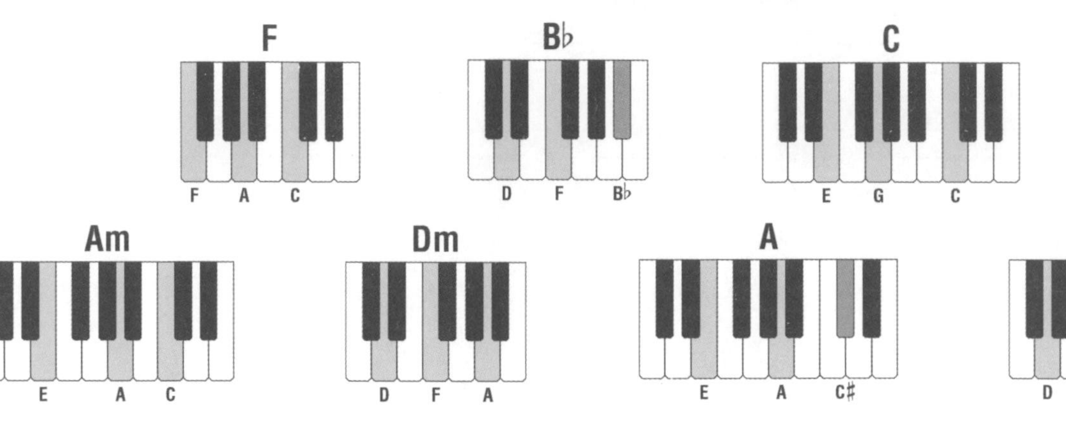

Words and Music by Elton John
and Bernie Taupin

Moderate Ballad

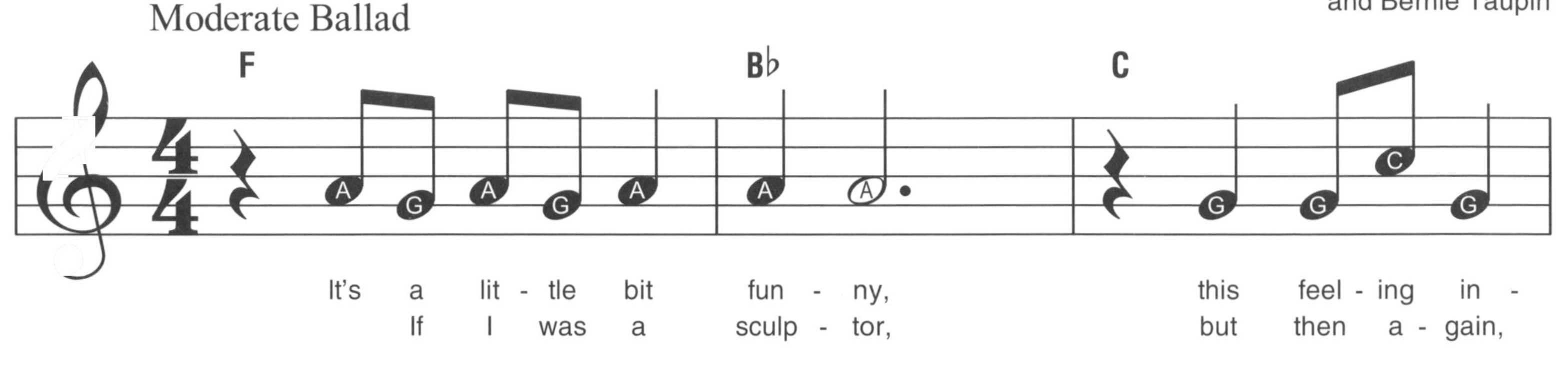

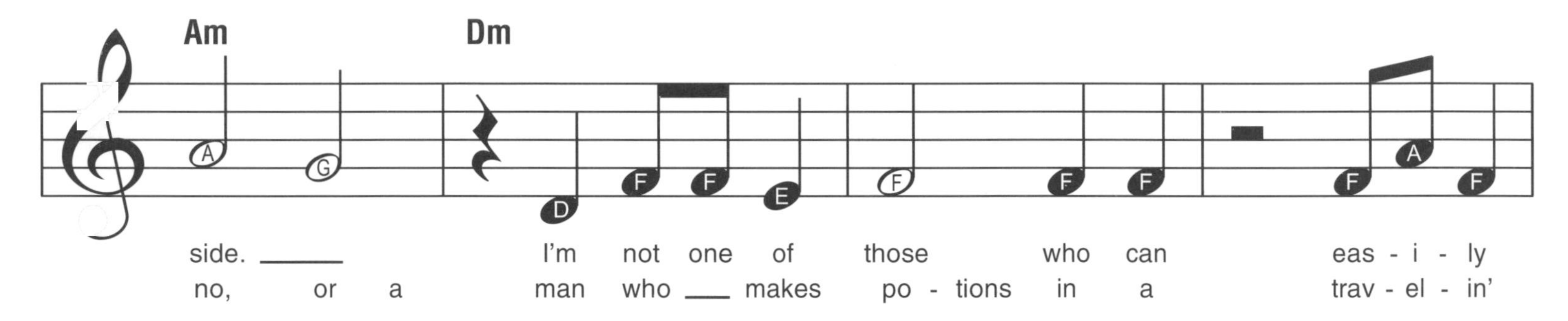

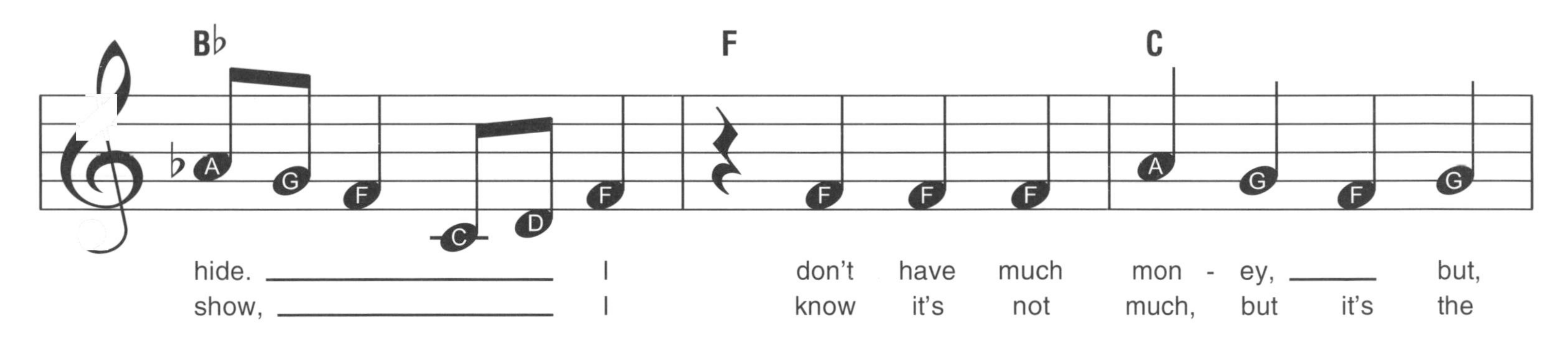

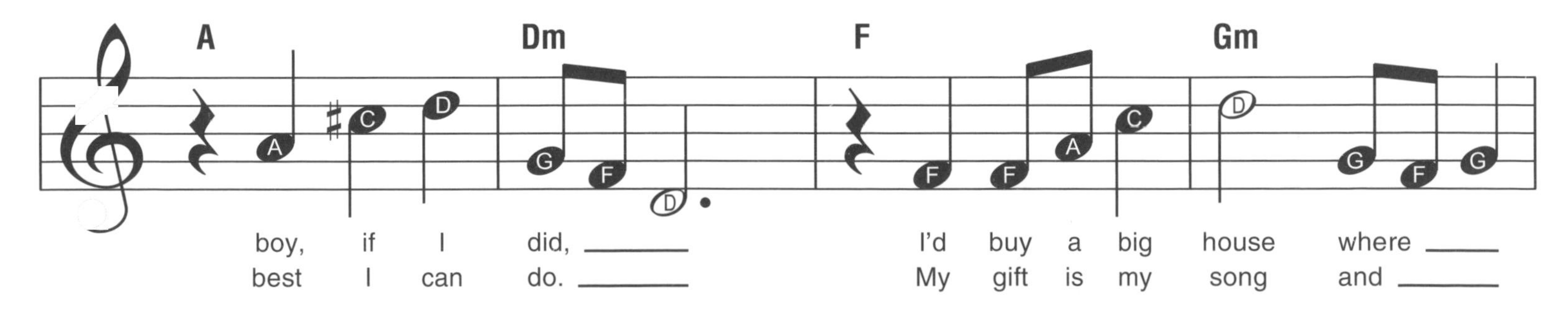

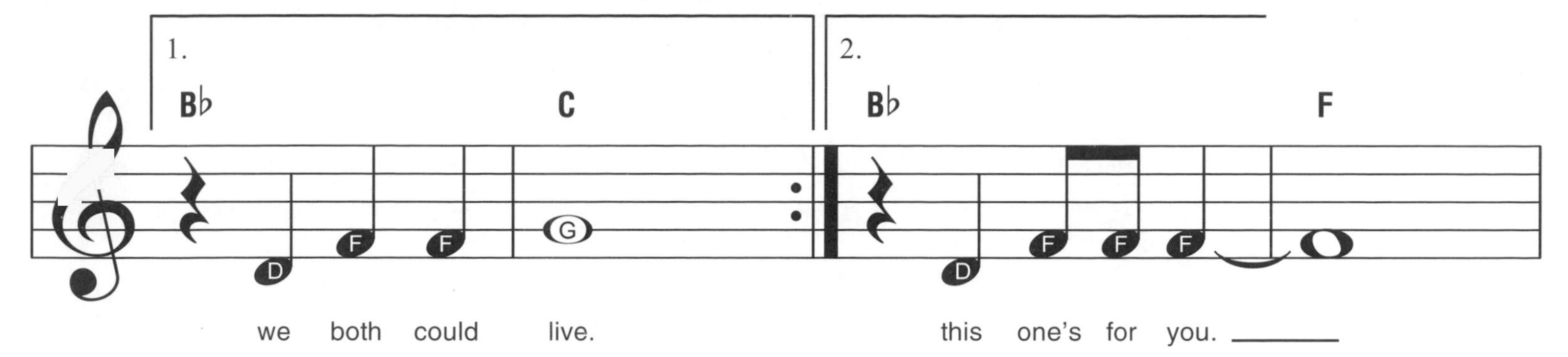
1.
2.
B♭
C
B♭
F
we both could live.
this one's for you.

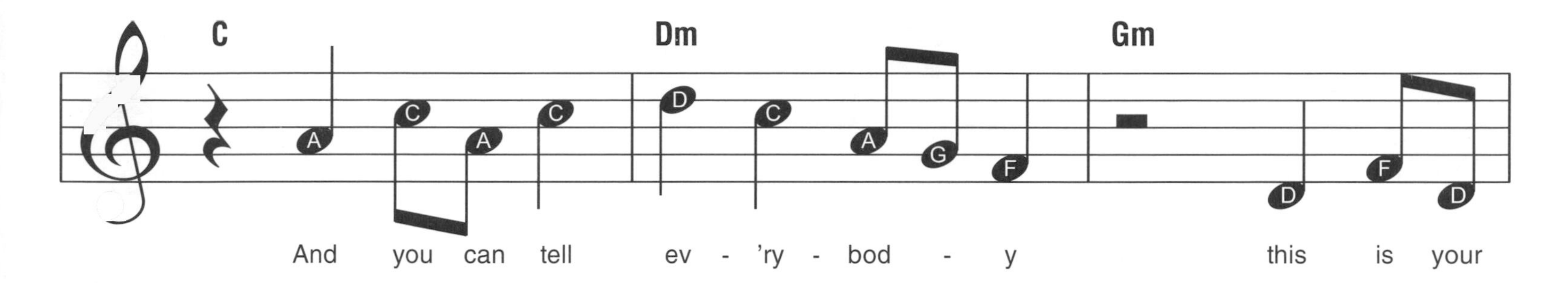
C
Dm
Gm
And you can tell ev - 'ry - bod - y this is your

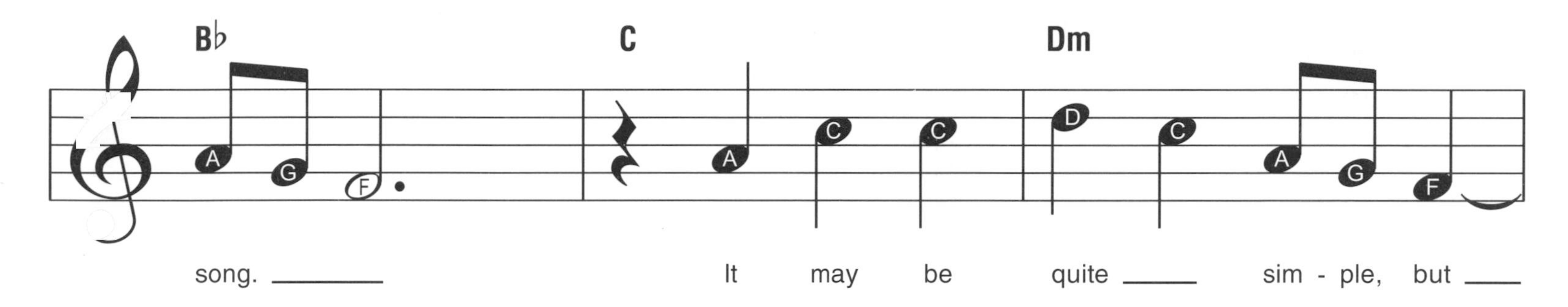
B♭
C
Dm
song. It may be quite sim - ple, but

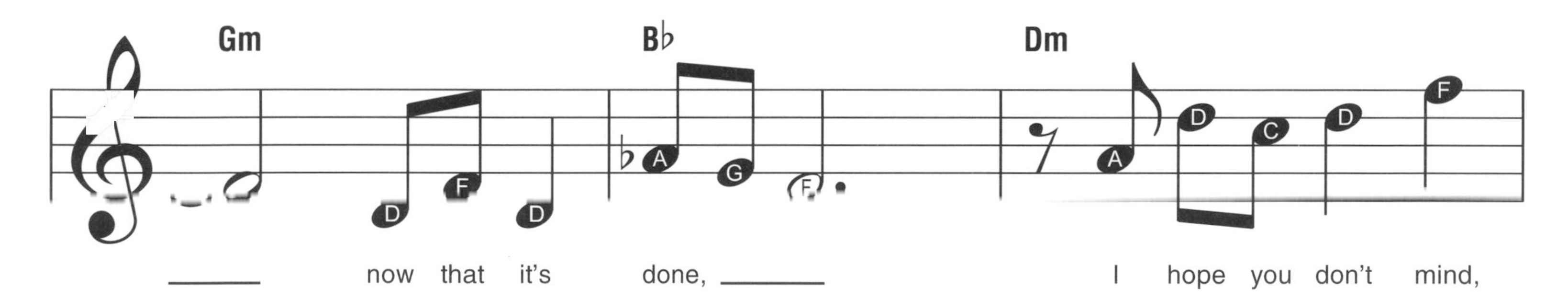
Gm
B♭
Dm
now that it's done, I hope you don't mind,

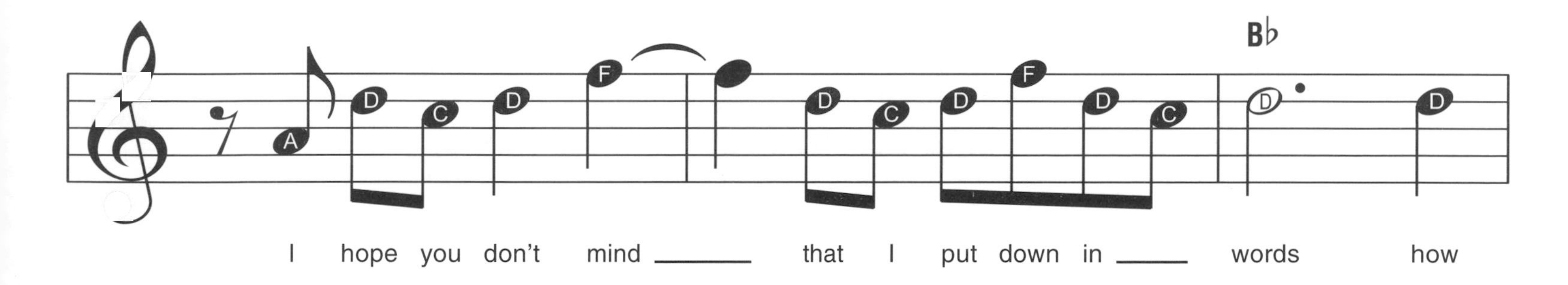
B♭
I hope you don't mind that I put down in words how

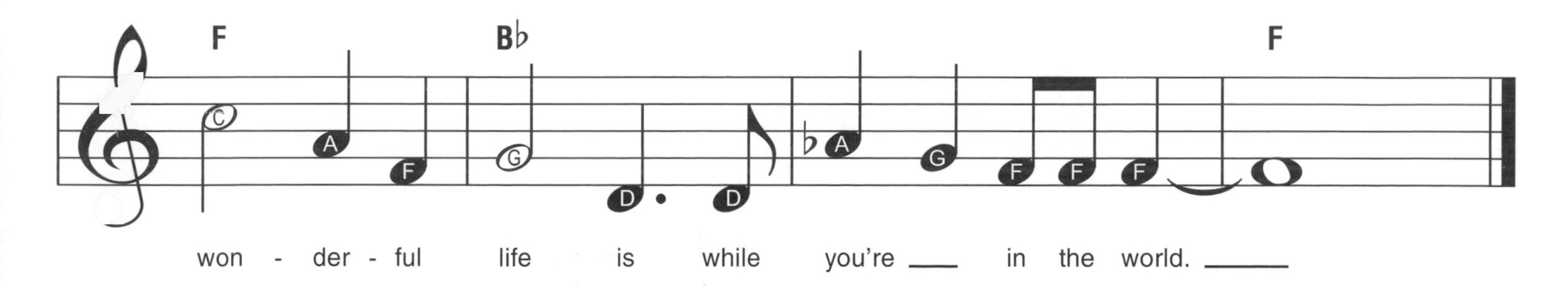
F
B♭
F
won - der - ful life is while you're in the world.

It's super easy! This series features accessible arrangements for piano, with simple right-hand melody, letter names inside each note, and basic left-hand chord diagrams. Perfect for players of all ages!

THE BEATLES
00198161 60 songs $15.99

BEAUTIFUL BALLADS
00385162 50 songs $14.99

BEETHOVEN
00345533 21 selections $9.99

BEST SONGS EVER
00329877 60 songs $15.99

BROADWAY
00193871 60 songs $15.99

JOHNNY CASH
00287524 20 songs $9.99

CHART HITS
00380277 24 songs $12.99

CHRISTMAS CAROLS
00277955 60 songs $15.99

CHRISTMAS SONGS
00236850 60 songs $15.99

CHRISTMAS SONGS WITH 3 CHORDS
00367423 30 songs $10.99

CLASSIC ROCK
00287526 60 songs $15.99

CLASSICAL
00194693 60 selections $15.99

COUNTRY
00285257 60 songs $15.99

DISNEY
00199558 60 songs $15.99

BOB DYLAN
00364487 22 songs $12.99

BILLIE EILISH
00346515 22 songs $10.99

FOLKSONGS
00381031 60 songs $15.99

FOUR CHORD SONGS
00249533 60 songs $15.99

FROZEN COLLECTION
00334069 14 songs $10.99

GEORGE GERSHWIN
00345536 22 songs $9.99

GOSPEL
00285256 60 songs $15.99

HIT SONGS
00194367 60 songs $15.99

HYMNS
00194659 60 songs $15.99

JAZZ STANDARDS
00233687 60 songs $15.99

BILLY JOEL
00329996 22 songs $10.99

ELTON JOHN
00298762 22 songs $10.99

KIDS' SONGS
00198009 60 songs $15.99

LEAN ON ME
00350593 22 songs $9.99

THE LION KING
00303511 9 songs $9.99

ANDREW LLOYD WEBBER
00249580 48 songs $19.99

MOVIE SONGS
00233670 60 songs $15.99

PEACEFUL MELODIES
00367880 60 songs $16.99

POP SONGS FOR KIDS
00346809 60 songs $16.99

POP STANDARDS
00233770 60 songs $15.99

QUEEN
00294889 20 songs $10.99

ED SHEERAN
00287525 20 songs $9.99

SIMPLE SONGS
00329906 60 songs $15.99

STAR WARS (EPISODES I-IX)
00345560 17 songs $10.99

TAYLOR SWIFT
00323195 22 songs $10.99

THREE CHORD SONGS
00249664 60 songs $15.99

TOP HITS
00300405 22 songs $10.99

WORSHIP
00294871 60 songs $15.99

Prices, contents and availability subject to change without notice.

0222
327